Teaching Palestine on an Israeli University Campus

Unsettling Denial

Daphna Golan-Agnon

Photographs Jack Persekian

Translation Janine Woolfson

ANTHEM PRESS

Anthem Press
An imprint of Wimbledon Publishing Company
www.anthempress.com

This edition first published in UK and USA 2021
by ANTHEM PRESS
75–76 Blackfriars Road, London SE1 8HA, UK
or PO Box 9779, London SW19 7ZG, UK
and
244 Madison Ave #116, New York, NY 10016, USA

British Library Cataloguing-in-Publication Data
A catalogue record for this book is available from the British Library.

Library of Congress Control Number: 2020946305

ISBN-13: 978-1-78527-501-2 (Hbk)
ISBN-10: 1-78527-501-1 (Hbk)
ISBN-13: 978-1-78527-504-3 (Pbk)
ISBN-10: 1-78527-504-6 (Pbk)

This title is also available as an e-book.

in memory
of Stanley Cohen,
a mentor and dear friend

CONTENTS

PHOTOGRAPHS BY JACK PERSEKIAN

ACKNOWLEDGMENTS

I am grateful to all the students who shared their stories with me and allowed me to share them with you. Aaron Back, representing the Ford Foundation, lent support to the Human Rights Fellowship program. He is also a close and generous friend who encouraged me to write this book. I am thankful for the ongoing support of the Minerva Center for Human Rights at the Hebrew University, and especially grateful to the Executive Director Danny Evron. Special thanks to the wonderful research assistants: Hala Mashood, Maya Vardi and Jiries Elias. I owe gratitude to the many colleagues and friends teaching, researching, evaluating, reflecting, acting and expanding Campus-Community partnerships and to our mentor Jonah Rosenfeld who led us down this path and graciously taught us to "learn from success." To Rema Hammami, many thanks for years of advising me on this book, for showing me how queer theory can be helpful when considering the legal situation of Palestinians in East Jerusalem, and for suggesting the title. The photography tour with Jack Persekian allowed me to discover new perspectives on, and from, the Mount Scopus campus where I have worked for some 30 years. I look forward to more joint trips. Thank you Janine Woolfson for a meticulous and sensitive translation, in which I can hear my own voice. Many thanks to the team of the Anthem Press—it has been a pleasure working with you.

Thank you Amotz Agnon, my lifelong partner. Thanks to my brilliant scholar-activist children Gali and Uri. I am so proud of you. It is my fervent wish that my wonderful grandchildren grow up to live in a land of peace and justice.

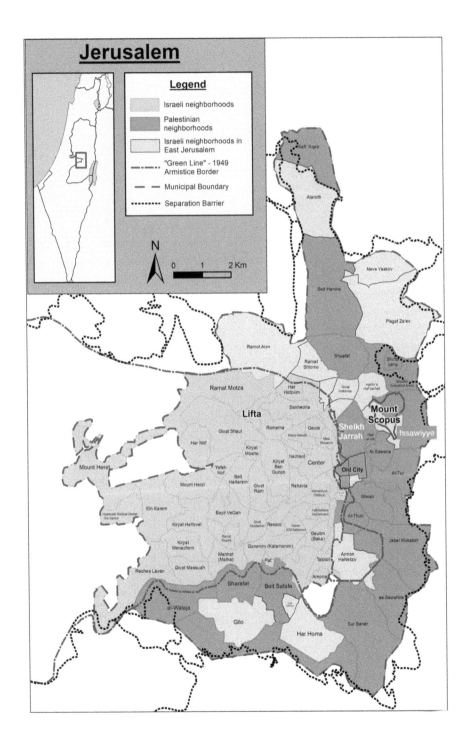

Map of Jerusalem

INTRODUCTION

In the second class of the year, a student named Tal asked me, "Why doesn't anybody talk about the war that's going on out there?" I redirected her question to the other students. We were sitting at a round table in a classroom on the Hebrew University of Jerusalem's Mount Scopus campus. The lesson hadn't begun yet and I was chopping cucumbers and helping set up the meal that one of the students had brought to share with the class. My students take turns preparing these suppers, which are always interesting and meaningful and, in most cases, delicious. "Why is nobody talking about the war that's going on out there?" I repeated. "Is there a war? Who isn't talking about it?"

The Minerva Human Rights Fellowship program in the Hebrew University's Faculty of Law admits outstanding students from across the university's departments. It was November 2000, the al Aqsa intifada was beginning,[1] but not one of the 16 students in the cohort had ever heard a lecturer mention, even in passing, "the war going on out there." The students were final year undergraduates or graduate students in international relations, law, Jewish thought, education, social work, and computer science. The disturbing events taking place off campus had not been acknowledged, let alone discussed, in any of their department.

I asked the students if *they* wanted to talk about it.

Six of the students in the group were Palestinian citizens of Israel. Just a few weeks earlier, 13 Palestinian citizens of Israel had been killed at a rally in support of the Palestinian popular uprising in the Occupied Territories. The conversation was slow to begin and palpably cautious. Given that the students in this diverse group did not yet know one another, the round table dictated the order of discussion, with each student speaking in turn. On that day, the Palestinian students asked if they could skip their turns.

The Jewish students expressed fear and frustration. They had come to Jerusalem from various parts of the country and they felt foreign in the cold, labyrinthine halls of this hilltop campus in the heart of East Jerusalem, far from the center of town. They spoke of feeling confused and of not having a space on campus in which to process this confusion. They all expressed

The tower

a desire to hear from the Palestinians. When the Palestinian students were eventually persuaded to speak, theirs was a story of twofold fear: the fear of bus bombings, which they shared with everyone, and the fear of being recognized as Arabs by other bus passengers terrified of bombings.

The question of why nobody discusses the war has arisen in every class since; the failure to acknowledge reality is pervasive, not unique to the Mount Scopus campus. This book will demonstrate the prevalence of political denial on all Israeli campuses. Nevertheless, the physical location of the Mount Scopus campus in the heart of Palestinian East Jerusalem makes this instance of denial particularly absurd. How on earth can reality be ignored when a student explains apologetically that she is late for class because the bus in front of the bus she was traveling on "blew up, so they closed the road and I had to walk"? How, when the smell of tear gas wafts into the classroom from in the nearby village of Issawiyye, can we carry on as if nothing is happening?

The campuses are political spaces and the decision not to address the "war out there" is as much a political statement as addressing it would be.

In spring 2017, at the behest of Education Minister Naphtali Bennet, Professor Assa Kasher published what he called an "ethical code for academia," which prohibits political discourse in campus classrooms. University officials and academics condemned this violation of freedom of speech, flooding academic platforms with objections, explaining the problematic nature of every item in the code. In an op-ed published in *Haaretz*,[2] I suggested that Professor Kasher should be thanked for instigating the stormy debate about freedom of expression currently taking place in Israeli academia.

Ironically, Kasher's code also reinforces the BDS movement's call for a boycott of Israeli academia because of its role in perpetuating the occupation. It envisions the self-censorship that already prevails on Israeli campuses being turned into an official ban. For years, Israeli academics have remained silent, for fear of saying something deemed inappropriate, and in doing so they have colluded with the disingenuous claim that the campuses are apolitical. Ministers and politicians regard the universities as leftist strongholds and endeavor to impose restraints on campus politics. As a result, the only political expressions permitted on campus at the moment are those in support of the government. In this absurd reality, inviting the Minister of Justice to speak at a graduation ceremony is not deemed a political act but mentioning the word "occupation" in the classroom most certainly is.

Every year, I come under personal attack from right-wing organizations like Im Tirzu, which claim that the human rights course I have been teaching for many years is politically biased. In December 2016, the Knesset Education Committee convened an emergency session entitled "Academic Courses against the State of Israel" to discuss charges leveled at my course by the

Association of Terror Victims. The intended outcome was to prohibit the universities from allowing students to intern with organizations that "support terrorism"—for example, the Association for Civil Rights in Israel.

This book is about the students in the Minerva Fellows for Human Rights class, a different group each year, who shook me to the core. The program, which operates in the Faculty of Law, requires students to commit to interning in human rights organizations once or twice a week in addition to the theoretical study of human rights and Israeli society. This is a bona fide academic full-year course, with credits, readings and a final paper; it is not a "Jewish-Arab dialogue" group. I participated in dozens of such dialogue forums in the 1980s and moderated many of them in the 1990s. Those experiences prompted me to address the asymmetry that inheres in these dialogues in the context of the occupation by attempting to explain why Israeli and Palestinian women never shared meals in the years we operated the Jerusalem Link.[3] Given this perspective, I was determined to design a course that was as far removed from a dialogue group as possible.

The students in each cohort are selected from a variety of backgrounds and academic disciplines, including medicine, law, social work, and international relations. The majority of them are women, about a third of them Palestinian women. This book aims to share what I have learned from these students, every one of whom has expressed gratitude for this unique and unprecedented opportunity to interact and learn from one another.

The first chapter orients the reader on the Mount Scopus campus, situated in the heart of East Jerusalem, and explores the silencing that prevails there. Chapters 2, 3, and 4 take the form of a tour of the Palestinian communities surrounding the campus: Issawiyye, Sheikh Jarrah, and Lifta. The tour begins in the enchanting botanical gardens on the Mount Scopus campus, moving beyond the sacred carob tree that stands in the neighboring village of Issawiyye, a 10-minute walk from the university. The chapter describes how Minerva students established a youth club in Issawiyye. This was the first time that these students, who were Palestinian citizens of Israel, members of the Palestinian elite, had encountered Palestinian villagers living under occupation. Working with Palestinian children who had never seen the sea, or even a swimming pool, caused them to consider their own Palestinian identity in new ways.

Chapter 3 takes us to Sheikh Jarrah, a neighborhood bordering the campus. Here, after four decades of legal procedures, the Israeli courts gave the police mandate to evict four Palestinian families from their homes so that Jewish settlers could occupy them. The students who were involved in the struggle for Palestinian rights in Sheikh Jarrah were forced to examine the nature of "justice."[4]

Chapter 4 sets out from the Lifta falafel stand, tucked between the student dorms and a cluster of houses that belong to refugees who had fled Lifta in 1948. Along with the students, we'll walk down to the abandoned village of Lifta, on the outskirts of Jerusalem. For me, Lifta embodies the hope for reconciliation.

Chapter 5 takes us back to the classroom on Mount Scopus, where we try to understand what it was that facilitated dialogue and sharing among the students in this program. We will linger on the effective combination of learning and action that facilitated this dialogue among young people willing to commit to changing the status quo.

The sixth and final chapter deals with the meals the students shared and the modicum of comfort that food can offer, provided the growing challenges and obstacles that keep Israelis and Palestinians from interacting are acknowledged.

Chapter 1

THE MOUNT SCOPUS CAMPUS

Individuals who tended to respond only to what was created to be useful to man were astonished by what they saw from Mount Scopus: the city, the Temple Mount, the wilderness inhabited by infinite colors, the Dead Sea, whose quiet blue flows up from the bottom of the deep, capped by hills and valleys that soar and dip and wrinkle, with every wind etching shapes above like those below, from which a breeze ripples upward and flutters overhead.

—S. Y. Agnon, *Shira*[1]

Everything that makes up a normal university was in place at Mount Scopus—students, courses, reading lists, libraries, departments, faculties—but every so often I had the vaguely paranoid feeling that things were not quite right. I was relieved to find out that this was not my own autistic fantasies. Visitors and newcomers would also sometimes get the feeling that these were virtual universities; that they were on a Hollywood set and would wake up the next morning to find everything removed, the whole place empty. It felt like an elaborately crafted movie in which there was no occupation, no intifada, and the university was set in New Zealand.

—Stanley Cohen, "The Virtual Reality of Universities in Israel"[2]

The Mount Scopus campus of the Hebrew University is perched atop Jerusalem's highest mountain. Every day, hundreds of tourists traverse the campus, stopping to take in views of the Old City, the Judean desert and, on especially clear days, the Dead Sea. The breathtaking vistas, however, are not visible from inside the fortress-like campus. There are very few places, such as the veranda of the faculty club and the window of the synagogue, that afford (spectacular) overviews of the Old City. The campus, which turns its back on the surrounding world, is often referred to disparagingly as the fortress, the labyrinth, or the bunker.

The notion of establishing a university in Jerusalem first appeared on the agenda of the World Zionist Organization in 1913. The cornerstone was laid in July 1918 and the Mount Scopus campus was inaugurated in 1925. The founders of the Hebrew University envisioned a center of learning for the entire Jewish people. Chaim Weizmann, the progenitor of the institution, declared at the cornerstone ceremony that it would be a center for the revival of Jewish thought, a focal point for Jews of the diaspora, a magnet for the best of Jewish youth and a tool for preparing and promoting settlement.[3] Judah Leon Magnes, a well-known Reform rabbi from the United States, an influential pacifist and a supporter of the idea of a binational Arab–Jewish state, was the founding president of the Hebrew University. Other renowned intellectuals like Gershom Scholem, Ernest Akiva Simon, and Martin Buber were among the faculty.

The campus was built on Mount Scopus—at a remove from the city's Jewish neighborhoods. The only way to reach it was through the neighborhood of Sheikh Jarrah. In 1945, the Hadassah Medical Center, affiliated with the Hebrew University, was opened near the campus. Strategically, the mount dominates its surroundings. Members of the Haganah trained there and it housed the central weapons armories of the Jerusalem District. The Haganah's science corps developed weaponry in the university's laboratories and there was a communications post atop one of the buildings that transmitted light signals to the Dead Sea area.[4]

At the beginning of January 1948, the Haganah bombed the Muslim Council building in Sheikh Jarrah. Studies were suspended at the Mount Scopus campus and the Jewish families who lived in the neighborhood were evacuated to West Jerusalem. In April 1948, Arab forces attacked a convoy headed for the besieged Mount Scopus. Seventy-seven people were killed, 24 of them medical professionals from Hadassah Hospital and 17 of them associated with the university. In July of that year, a demilitarization agreement was signed, which designated the campus an enclave under Israeli sovereignty and United Nations protection. The Jordanians, who controlled East Jerusalem, made the university's continued operation contingent on the return of Palestinian refugees. This demand was not met[5] and the campus remained closed after the war. Studies were relocated to Terra Sancta and other locations in West Jerusalem and the Mount Scopus campus became a military command post. From 1948 to 1967, the campus was an Israeli military stronghold within an Israeli enclave (that included the village of Issawiyye) inside Jordanian territory. In 1958, a new campus was inaugurated at the West Jerusalem site of Givat Ram, which houses the natural science faculties to this day.

Immediately after the 1967 war and the conquest of Jerusalem, the standing committee of the Hebrew University senate decided that reviving the Mount Scopus campus and reinstating activities on the site was a matter of great importance and urgency.[6] The university appointed a committee to undertake the relocation of part of the university to Mount Scopus, with the understanding that "the transition was to be genuine and not merely symbolic, requiring relocation of large units such as entire faculties."[7] It was decided that massive land appropriation would be necessary as the campus was restored and expanded. To ensure that the trauma of losing Mount Scopus in 1948 never recur, it was deemed necessary to create a territorial continuum of Jewish neighborhoods all the way to West Jerusalem.

And indeed, on January 11, 1968, the Ministry of Justice issued the first postwar land appropriation order: 3,830 dunams[8] (some 950 acres) in north-eastern Jerusalem were appropriated to expand the Mount Scopus campus and build the neighborhoods of French Hill, Ammunition Hill, Maalot Dafna, and Ramat Eshkol. These neighborhoods came to be referred to as the "gateway neighborhoods" because they constituted Jewish Israeli territorial continuity from Sanhedria in West Jerusalem to Mount Scopus.

The university's leadership was actively involved in the campus expansion and the demand for land appropriation, as attested to by minutes of standing committee meetings from that time. Haim Yacobi emphasizes that the university regarded the area as "terra nullius"[9]—a colonialist term for territory not subject to any sovereignty. The residents of Lifta and Issawiyye, from whom lands were seized, received no mention at the standing committee's meetings.

The president of the university expressed pride in the institution's role as the primary settlement in east Jerusalem: "The development of our compound is the principal project in the settlement and population of East Jerusalem. Tens, hundreds of millions of lira [pounds] will be invested in this endeavor which will draw thousands of students to East Jerusalem, many of whom will live on and around Mount Scopus. Is there a greater project anywhere?"[10] The construction of the Jewish neighborhoods isolated Issawiyye from the neighboring Palestinian neighborhoods and from the Old City and significantly reduced the area of the village. Issawiyye became an impoverished neighborhood of East Jerusalem, with almost no land zoned for development.

The university leadership's enthusiasm for returning to Mount Scopus was aligned with the government's perception of students and lecturers who would teach and study on Mount Scopus as "the population of a small city, part of the ribbon of new neighborhoods in east Jerusalem." The prevailing view was that a large number of students living on campus would constitute a kind of "garrison" that could, if necessary, prevent a repeat of the 1947–48 situation.[11]

Construction of the gateway neighborhoods of French Hill and Ramat Eshkol began as early as 1969. Their purpose was not only to create a territorial continuum between West Jerusalem and Mount Scopus but also to separate the Old City from the Palestinian neighborhoods to its north. Nir Hasson explains that this was the beginning of a "pattern that Israel has yet to shake off: the goal of building in Jerusalem is not to meet the needs of the city and its inhabitants, but part of a political struggle—punishment for the other side, declaration of ownership, acts of protest, or part of a strategic view based primarily on land acquisition and Judaisation of the area."[12]

In 1981, the rebuilt campus was inaugurated. At its center is a tower, a concrete representation of Israeli control over Jerusalem. A wall surrounds the entire campus.[13] The design aligns with the central concept of the campus' architects, namely that it is "in dialogue with the Old City, resonating with its walls."[14] Diana Dolev has described the architecture of the new campus as a "megastructure that communicates aggression toward the surroundings it dominates, policing those within as well."[15] Students often joke about the labyrinthine campus and the legends of people lost in its bowels for years. In her novel *I am Leona*, Gail Hareven describes the thoughts of a girl arriving at the Mount Scopus campus for the first time.

> It was not a beautiful place; it barely had any windows. The air from outside was not allowed in, and walls obscured the view of Jerusalem. My incredulity increased by the moment, but I told myself that perhaps there was a secret to this, that there must be a hidden reason for the way the fortress was constructed. Those who devote themselves to the intellect, I thought, probably need to distance themselves from the chaos of the city, forswear even its beauty lest they be distracted from their studies.[16]

Today, most students access the campus via the Jewish neighborhoods of French Hill and Ramat Eshkol. The vast majority of them are unaware that these neighborhoods were constructed after 1967 in what had previously been East Jerusalem. Neither they nor the university's faculty encounter Palestinians as they make their way to the campus. The green Israeli buses stop in a tunnel inside the campus. The white buses that transport Palestinian students drive around the back of the campus, dropping their passengers outside the walls of—the best university in Israel and one of the leading academic institutions in the world.

The Rules of Campus Discourse: What Not to Say

Michal Frenkel, a sociologist and professor at the Hebrew University, writes about taboos in the classroom. She describes her attempt to "find out what cannot be spoken of in the classroom if everyone wants to make it home safely. An attempt, as a sociologist, to understand why I myself conform to the mechanisms of control and censorship, even though they constitute a profound violation of my professional identity."[17] Frenkel describes how she silences and censors herself as a result of student responses: " 'Politics aside' is the most frequently used phrase in recordings that could serve as damning evidence," she writes, referring obliquely to the recordings of lectures made furtively by Im Tirzu activists to provide supporting evidence for their accusations of inappropriate political content. "As sociologists, we are well aware that depoliticization is itself a type of politics," Frenkel clarifies. Nevertheless, in the classroom, Frenkel "avoids conflict, qualifies every provocative statement, or apologizes in advance for any potential offense to any of the students," all the while feeling as if she is "seriously violating her commitment to the discipline of sociology and her students." She asks, "What is it that checks the lecturer from expressing every idea she has, be it the most provocative?" and answers:

> There is a clear price to pay for disturbing the students' complacency. The department, faculty and university's increasing dependence on enrollment numbers, and competition with less demanding alternative institutions, necessitates increasing concern with student satisfaction at the expense of challenging the obvious and fostering subversive and innovative thinking [...] So she [the lecturer] walks on eggs, thinks twice about every sentence, represses evidence and holds two heartfelt hopes: the first is that something of her own disturbed complacency will nevertheless be communicated to the students and disturb theirs, and the second is that years of self-censorship, internalization of mechanisms of control and fear of provocativeness, will not make her too complacent as well.[18]

It is telling that Frenkel manages to recount, with admirable candor, the self-silencing and censorship that prevails on Mount Scopus without once mentioning the occupation—that most significant subject that is rarely mentioned and never taught on Israeli campuses.

The discussion of what can and cannot be spoken of on the Hebrew University campus is exemplified by three different encounters I had during the 2013–14 academic year. They are described below, in illustration of what happens on campus when one dares utter the word "occupation."

View toward the Dead Sea

"States of Denial" in the School of Social Work

In the fall of 2013, I was invited to deliver a guest lecture to a group of grad-uate students in the School of Social Work. I assigned reading the introduction to Stanley Cohen's book *States of Denial: Knowing about Atrocities and Suffering* in advance.[19] Cohen recounts his first political memory as a boy growing up in South Africa in the 1950s. He recalls how, on a particularly cold night, before he went to bed, he looked out of the window and saw the night guard trying to warm his hands by a fire he had lit in the yard. "Why should this old man have to sit out in the cold all night?" was one of the questions Cohen recalls asking. "Why has our family (and everyone like us) been allocated black men and women (who were called 'boys' and 'girls' or just 'natives') as domestic servants? Why do they live in tiny rooms in the backyard?" A few years later, Cohen began asking a different question:

> Why did others, even those raised in similar families, schools and neighborhoods, who read the same papers, walked the same streets, apparently not "see" what we saw? Could they be living in another per-ceptual universe—where the horrors of apartheid were invisible and the physical presence of black people often slipped from awareness? Or perhaps they saw *exactly* what we saw, but just didn't care or didn't see anything wrong.[20]

For years, Cohen collected studies, news articles, and brochures dealing with how people respond to evidence of inflicted suffering. He examined the questions: What do we do with the knowledge of the suffering of others? What does this knowledge do to us? During the years he spent in Jerusalem teaching in the faculty of law's criminology institute, Cohen began writing about the "sociology of denial." This was in response to reactions elicited by a report that he and I coauthored for B'Tselem: "The Interrogation of Palestinians During the Intifada: Ill-treatment, 'Moderate Physical Pressure' or Torture?"[21] The report, which was published in 1991, presented the standard forms of torture used by Israel daily in military and police interrogations. It showed that most Palestinians who were detained were severely tortured. Media cov-erage was extensive and two commissions of inquiry were convened to study the findings: one by the military and one by the ministry of justice and the security services. It was the first time a discussion of this taboo subject was tabled and the responses led Cohen to discern that there were different types of denial.

Cohen was particularly perturbed by how liberal Israelis, particularly academics, failed to take action. He wrote about their strategies of avoidance and denial: "I wanted to say 'Don't you know what's happening?' the entire time. But, of course, they knew. This was another example of denial, not crude and cynical lies but the complex conundrum of people trying not to notice what was happening so that they could seem innocent."[22]

Some 40 students attended the session. I asked them to share instances of denial they knew of or had experienced. One student suggested that every time we eat chicken, we are in denial about the fact that it is a dead bird. Another noted that we continue to drive even though we know there is a possibility we will be in an accident.

We discussed Cohen's theory that there are different stages of denial: *literal denial* in which the fact, or the knowledge of the fact, are denied (it didn't happen; they're all liars; my partner could not do that to our child; there was no massacre); *interpretive denial*, in which it is acknowledged that something happened, but it is given a different interpretation (Bill Clinton did not have sexual relations with Monica Lewinsky; it wasn't ethnic cleansing but population transition; this is not torture, it's moderate physical pressure; what happened is not what you say it is); *implicatory denial*, in which the facts and their standard interpretation are acknowledged, but the psychological, political, and moral ramifications are denied (what can we do?; someone will take care of it; it's not my problem; things are worse in other places). These are all ways we use to justify and rationalize, cope (or not cope) with the knowledge of suffering.

I asked the students to think about what else we deny. One student asked if I was referring to what we are doing to the Palestinians. I asked her to elaborate but she refused. "Do you mean the occupation?" I asked. "What occupation?" asked another student. "How can you say occupation?" said another. "That's taking a political stance," complained another. All the students concurred that they had never heard the word "occupation" spoken on campus. Not on the Mount Scopus campus in the heart of occupied East Jerusalem, nor on other campuses where they had been undergraduates. They were adamant that the word had no place on campus.

I explained that what Israeli law refers to as "administered" territories, conquered from Jordan and never deemed a sovereign entity, are considered Palestinian-Occupied Territories according to international law. But before I could finish explaining, a student who had not yet spoken asked for the floor, "When you say occupied, you mean that there are occupiers and occupied? Who is who in this case?" he asked. At this point, the lesson had run into overtime and I suggested that we continue the discussion one-on-one. But he and other students insisted: "How can you talk about the occupation? Who is occupied and who is the occupier here?"

Opening Event of the Academic Year: The Social Involvement Unit at the Hebrew University

The Hebrew University Social Involvement Unit's opening event of the academic year was scheduled for the last day of the festival of Hanukkah in 2013. Despite being ill, I braved the cold and torrential rain to attend, as I was to speak alongside Professor Yossi Yona from Ben Gurion University. Itzik Shmueli, a former chair of the student union who was elected to the Knesset after the 2011 social protests, was supposed to participate but did not attend. Yona (who has since been elected to parliament on the Zionist Camp ticket) spoke at length about his role as one of the expert advisors to the 2011 social protesters. He remarked that he feared the discussion would be dull as he was sure that he and I agreed on everything. I began by saying that I was not at all sure that was the case. I didn't linger on my role in that same struggle, the weeks I spent at the homeless tent camp in Jerusalem or my ongoing support for public housing for single mothers in Jerusalem. I didn't ask where the experts and protesting students disappeared when dozens of homeless families were left in tents with winter approaching. Instead, I suggested that a protest movement that claims to be apolitical and ignores the occupation is problematic.

The minute I said the word "occupation" there was a commotion. Three students demanded loudly that I not be allowed to continue, because I had used the forbidden word. Another student accused me of racism and several others threatened to disrupt my presentation or even the entire event. There were about 300 students in the hall and the symposium proceeded haltingly. As the event ended, I was approached by dozens of students, most of them Palestinians. "Do you teach here?" they asked. "How do you dare say such things? We've never heard anyone say the word 'occupation' on campus."

As the year progressed, I heard from many students that the incident continued to cause waves. They reiterated how shocked they had been to hear the word and how the question of whether the word "occupation" was permissible on campus continued to preoccupy the Social Involvement Unit for months.

Lesson One: Lafer Center Course on Feminism, Human Rights and Social Change

I began the lesson with the introduction to Judith Louise Herman's book *Trauma and Recovery*:

> It is very tempting to take the side of the perpetrator. All the perpetrator asks is that the bystander do nothing. He appeals to the universal

desire to see, hear and speak no evil. The victim, on the contrary, asks the bystander to share the burden of pain. The victim demands action, engagement, and remembering.[23]

Herman, a leading expert on trauma, writes about the solitude experienced by victims of sexual assault, who feel ashamed and silenced. She suggests that it was when trauma victims began organizing into groups that the first cracks appeared in the wall of social denial and victim-blaming, making acknowledgment of their trauma possible. One of the students in my class suggested that we are in denial about other things too, for example, the occupation. I asked her if she wanted to elaborate. There were 29 students in the room. Three doctoral students, ten graduate students, and several undergraduates. This was the first meeting of these students from different departments, of different ages, who were studying together at the Lafer Center for Women's and Gender Studies.

A law student sitting across from me raised his hand and blurted out, "You're not allowed to say 'occupation' in class!" I asked him why. "Because it's a political term; you are assuming a stance and that's against university policy." If the course had been geared only toward law students, I might have proceeded by asking exactly which laws govern the Occupied Territories, and why they do not fall under the jurisdiction of Israeli law. However, given that this was the first meeting of a very heterogeneous class, I suggested that we refer to the occupation as the "giraffe" and then directed the conversation toward a subject that is common to the feminist, human rights, and social change movements: naming and framing. I spoke about verbal definitions: words with constructed meanings and how the names we give to phenomena enable us to understand them. We discussed how naming/framing both reflects and constructs reality, for example, the connotative distinction between "family honor killing" and "spousal murder". Whole worlds of implicit assumptions are contained in these two appellations that, in the Israeli context, refer respectively to the murder of Arab women and the murder of Jewish women. I went on to speak about sexual harassment, a legal term that features regularly in the media and public discourse.

Student feedback after the lesson was plentiful. That evening, I received an email from Amira:

I've been a student at the Hebrew University for four years, but I've never been addressed or identified as Palestinian. I'm thinking about the importance of naming. I recognize that there's fear, hesitation, maybe even denial and opposition to acknowledging that we, Palestinian students at Hebrew University, are really Palestinians.

Another Palestinian student named Rawan wrote that not only was this the first time she had heard the word "occupation" on campus, but it was also the first time she had heard a Jew, a lecturer yet, say the word "Palestinian" on campus. She described how a Jewish student who approached her for Arabic lessons reacted to learning that she taught Palestinian Arabic. Horrified, she had asked, "But why Palestinian Arabic?" Rawan continued, "After I explained that I teach Palestinian Arabic because I am Palestinian, she insisted 'you are not Palestinian, you live in Israel; you are Arab'". Rawan's story illustrates the distinction that Jewish Israelis make between Palestinians in Jerusalem and the Occupied Territories—Palestinians versus "our Arabs", "Arab Israelis" or "Arab citizens of Israel"—an ideological one that most of the Palestinians on campus reject.

Israeli law does indeed distinguish between various groups of Palestinians, each of which has different rights: those who live in Jerusalem, the West Bank, Gaza, and Israel respectively. But it is particularly interesting that on a campus where Palestinian students define themselves as Palestinians, the Jewish students do not acknowledge this definition.

In their class feedback, several Jewish students explained at length why the word occupation should not be permitted on campus. One of these, a lawyer working on his Ph.D., wrote:

> My claim is not just that the terminology question (occupation or liberation) is irrelevant to human rights discourse, but that it is actually detrimental to it in the following way: When used in relation to people living in the Territories, the word "occupation" diverts the discussion from the main point, which is their human rights. The word, as we saw in the first meeting, instantaneously loads the discussion politically, religiously, and emotionally and effectively prevents authentic and vital discussion of the rights of residents of the Territories.

He went on in this vein, but without elucidating what that "authentic and vital discussion" would be. He did not mention the word Palestinian, nor offer an alternative to the word "occupation". He also made no suggestions regarding how to change the reality that he refused to call an occupation.

In light of the volume of feedback I received after this lesson, I began the next session by asking the students to express the feelings they had brought to class that day. The discussion was heated and I struggled to moderate between students seeking to express their confusion, report arguments they had had with friends and family, and raise questions that emerged from the previous lesson. The student who had written to me at length about why the use of the word "occupation" was illegitimate, explained his view that the word was divisive and alienating—an obstacle to discussion. Some of his classmates responded with annoyance, suggesting sardonically, "Perhaps we shouldn't talk about rape because the word is divisive and alienating. Perhaps we should just say that something bad happened, or focus on the human rights of the victim.". Some of the female students spoke about the cost of silencing and being silenced. They described their experiences of the latter in terms of violence, noting that the Hebrew words for violence and muteness come from the same root.

I had not intended to devote the entire lesson to the occupation but, as I am becoming increasingly aware, the word itself evokes strong feelings for all students: those who have never heard it in the classroom and do not acknowledge its existence; those who have never heard the word in class but know that some people use it; those who are active against the occupation but have nevertheless never heard it spoken in class; and the Palestinian students who don't understand how there can be Jews who don't know about the occupation—how anyone who had spent their military service in the Territories could conceivably deny it.

Everybody wanted to discuss whether or not, and how, and when, and where, we should talk about the occupation.

I did not say much during the lesson. I was trying to memorize the students' names, make sure everyone had a turn to speak and limit those who went on too long. I didn't say a word about the human rights situation in the Occupied Territories, but after the lesson I got a lot of feedback from students who claimed that we had not spent enough time discussing the Jewish people's existential fear, the "fear that we are the persecuted nation who face eradication in every generation." One graduate student wrote: "Being open to using the word 'occupation', in our society, opens up an array of connotations: leftism, naiveté, Arab-loving, defilement of Israel. Open use of the word 'occupation' puts every individual's existence at risk." She did not explain why she found the term so threatening, but assumed that she shared her fear with everyone. And what was it she was afraid of? Open use of the word "occupation". This student expressed fear, shared with many of her peers, not of the occupation itself — or the implications of 50 years of military rule over another people—but of talking about it.

The voices of all these students—the graduate student of social work who asked me, "If there is such a thing as an occupation, who is occupying and who is being occupied?"; the student who regarded use of the term as a threat to all Israelis and an endangering of their existence; the Ph.D. law student who

View from new gate

insisted that the word is divisive and alienating, were begging to be heard. In addition to their criticism, shock, and fear at the very mention of the word, all the students admitted to never having discussed "it" on campus. The vast majority of them wanted to. "If there is an occupation," they asked, "why has no one ever spoken to us about it? Not at school, not in the army, not at home, and not at university. Nobody talks about the occupation. If there's an occupation, then are we, the only democracy in the Middle East, the democratic Jewish country, really occupiers?"

Yehuda Shenhav has shown that a negligible number of Israeli sociologists have publicly expressed opposition to the occupation and that "most Israeli sociologists almost completely ignore the occupation as a relevant working paradigm."[24] He argues that "neutrality" or "scientific objectivity" positions intellectuals and scientists outside the discussion of the most important questions of the day.

Writing this book on the 50th anniversary of the occupation, I suggest extrapolating Shenhav's position to characterizing the silence, the failure to mention the occupation, on campus as not only a betrayal of the intellectual's role, but an active perpetuation of the situation. The academic community's failure to acknowledge the occupation and express opposition to it is one of the main reasons we are still discussing whether or not it exists rather than seeking ways to end it. By not speaking of the occupation, by not facilitating discussion and action directed at ending it, we have unwittingly strengthened the growing camp that denies its existence. This is the camp that governs Israel today. It claims that the entire land of Israel belongs to the Jewish people and that Israel is not an occupier because it was promised the land by God.

By choosing to remain silent, academics collude with the regime to erase the Green Line from maps and consciousness, appropriate Palestinian lands, build Jewish settlements in the Occupied Territories, oppress the Palestinian population by military rule, and pretend that it is all temporary, "not so bad" and, definitely, not an appropriate subject for discussion in the classroom.

Ignoring the occupation as if it does not exist teaches students that there are issues—even ones central to our lives and our future—that are best not discussed on campus since we are helpless to do anything about them. This is a defeatist message: surrender to the power of the regime, surrender to the increasingly pervasive Israeli narrative of dominance and control. Failure to discuss the occupation diverts the perceptions of young Israelis away from international law and the prevailing global sentiment that the occupation must be stopped.

According to international law all of the territories conquered in 1967, which Israel refers to as the "administered areas", are occupied Palestinian territories. In all of them, including east Jerusalem, Palestinians live under occupation, a situation that should have been temporary, ending shortly after the war.

In 1949, after the horrors of the Second World War and the murder of millions of citizens, the four Geneva Conventions were adopted. These international treaties dictate two basic wartime principles: differentiation between combatants and civilians, and proportional use of weapons. The first three treaties deal with combatants who are no longer active: the wounded, sick, or shipwrecked. Such people still have basic rights: medical care, food and return home after the conflict has ended. The Fourth Geneva Convention is meant to ensure that civilian genocide of the kind that happened in World War II never recurs. The treaty defines the population in occupied territories as "protected persons" whose rights and laws must be respected by the occupier. Occupation is meant to be a temporary state and any changes made in occupied territories must be in the interests of the protected population.

According to international humanitarian law, all the settlements, including the Jewish neighborhoods in east Jerusalem, are illegal.

But let me return to the campus in an attempt to understand the students' terror at the very mention of the word "occupation". It is no wonder they struggle to accept the reality of the occupation: the government of Israel denies it; a state commission of inquiry headed by Justice (emeritus) Edmond Levi declared it non-existent. Even the Supreme Court, the bastion of Israeli liberalism, will not use the phrase Occupied Territories (as determined by international law and used worldwide), instead, referring nebulously to "the area". The minister of culture demands that the arts community stop talking about the occupation; teachers and parents never, ever, mention it. No wonder.

Some of the students that I met in the scenarios described above not only object vehemently to the word "occupation" being uttered on campus, but remain convinced that the occupation does not exist. Unfortunately, as I will proceed to demonstrate, this is also the position adopted by most lecturers, who just want to "make it home safely", and the implicit position of the leaders of higher education who continue to insist that their institutions are apolitical.

Im Tirzu's emphatic urging of students to record lectures and thus ensure that no challenges to the consensus are voiced in the classroom is, sadly, the prevailing norm on campus. Minister of Education Naphtali Benet deems any political expression that is not pro-government unacceptable. This aligns with the ethical code developed by "court philosopher" Assa Kasher. Those who deny the occupation defend their right—vociferously and threateningly— to not hear other positions. Two principal misapprehensions inhere in this approach: The first is that the military occupation of the territories is an invention, or political opinion, when it is, in fact, a reality that Palestinians and Israelis, for that matter the whole world, have been dealing with for over 50 years. The Palestinian territories are governed by the Israeli military. Military orders, military courts, and IDF soldiers are, for the most part, in charge of Palestinians entering and exiting the occupied areas and they effectively control the lives of millions of Palestinians. I will not elaborate on the factual inaccuracy inherent in this misapprehension.

The second misapprehension is that the university is not political and that mentioning the occupation is a violation of this apolitical condition.

The Hebrew University's first communiqué with faculty and students during the Israeli bombardment of Gaza (Operation Protective Edge) in the summer of 2014, began by announcing that a fundraising drive for students called up to serve was doing well and gaining momentum. A letter from the chair of the student union, Major (reserves) Eldad Postan, was included. Postan described being called upon the very first day of Operation Protective Edge and hurrying to the army base because "we must do what we are called upon to do". In a video message that the university president sent to faculty and students some days later, he again stressed the importance of the university's support for the troops, mentioning a campaign to send food and supply packages to soldiers on the front.

The university's unequivocal support for the pointless and destructive war in Gaza was especially astounding given its righteous claims to apolitical status and freedom of thought and expression. It reflected the prevailing view that while support for the military and government policy is not political, opposition to them most certainly is. The majority of lecturers and students accept this distinction between "apolitical" support for the regime and "unacceptable political" opposition to said regime. How ironic that dissemination of a letter signed by an army general about reporting for reserve duty, or indeed war itself, are "without a doubt" not political activities, but mentioning the word occupation on campus is.

Of course, the Hebrew University was not alone in its unequivocal support for this futile war. At the end of June 2014, Professor Hanoch Sheinman, who teaches in the Faculty of Law at Bar Ilan University, sent his students a letter to inform them of a change in the exam schedule necessitated by the "security situation", i.e. the war in Gaza. He included his hope that all were "in a safe place, and that you, your families and those dear to you are not among the hundreds of people that have been killed, the thousands wounded, or the tens of thousands whose homes have been destroyed or who have been forced to leave their homes during, or as a direct result of, the violent confrontation in the Gaza Strip and its environs". Students issued a complaint to the dean of the faculty Professor Shahar Lifshitz, claiming that the letter was offensive.[25] In response to such complaints, Lifshitz issued the following statement:

> Both the content and the style of the letter contravene the values of the university and the faculty of law. The faculty champions the values of pluralism, tolerance, and freedom of expression, but the inclusion of positions such as those included in the administrative message sent by Prof. Sheinman to the students on a matter relating to exams does not fit the framework of academic freedom or freedom of personal expression in any acceptable sense. This constitutes inappropriate use of the power given to a lecturer. He exploited the platform given to him as a law teacher to convey messages reflecting his positions in a way that, as noted, seriously offended the students and their families.

The students' furious and offended responses to their teacher including the Palestinian wounded, dead, and displaced, in his message, even if only by intimation, were very disturbing. Even more disturbing, however, was the university's unequivocal support for the complainants and public condemnation of the lecturer, who was accused of betraying the university's values.

It is taken for granted that Israeli institutions of higher education support the military. The campuses house military, strategic and security-related institutes, programs and study centers that facilitate classified research undertakings in coordination with the security services. In many academic institutions, there are abbreviated academic degree programs designed exclusively for military personnel. Many scholarships and other benefits are available for student veterans and reserves. The Hebrew University has a separate tenure track for researchers working with the security forces. Some of the research is classified and the tenure and promotion committees are precluded from reviewing it. These are all important issues that do not get enough academic and public attention. University support for the army is so obvious to university officials as well as most employees and students that they do not regard it as a political statement at all.

Professor Zeev Sternhell, an international expert on fascism, made the following statements about the Gaza war in an interview for *Haaretz*:

> What we've seen here in the past few weeks is absolute conformism on the part of most of Israel's intellectuals. They've just followed the herd. By intellectuals, I mean professors and journalists. The intellectual bankruptcy of the mass media in this war is total. It's not easy to go against the herd, you can easily be trampled. But the role of the intellectual and the journalist is not to applaud the government. Democracy crumbles

when the intellectuals, the educated classes, toe the line of the thugs or look at them with a smile.[26]

But even Sternhell qualifies this criticism by noting that he "does not have enough military knowledge". The recent war, he says, "was absolutely an optional one, disorganized and fly by night...something had to be done the moment they started firing. ...The rockets had to be countered. Could it have been stopped without the massive intervention of the airforce? I don't know. I do not have enough military knowledge. I no longer have friends in the military."[27]

Academics are meant to challenge and critique ties between the academy and the military. In Israel, however, the reciprocity between the academy and the army or security services is perceived as an ineluctable fact.

To ignore the military occupation and support military and government policy are perceived in Israeli discourse—and the academic arena—as apolitical. To criticize government policy, or even mention the military occupation, is considered political and illegitimate. Self-censorship along with frequent threats from Im Tirzu and government representatives demanding that lecturers who do not comply be dismissed, are part of the general atmosphere on campus, where critical politics is unwelcome.

In December 2010 the Council for Higher Education published a directive according to which "All attempts to politicize the academy should be rejected. The council asserts that academic freedom is complete freedom to research and consider and, concerning the students, the institution's responsibility is to strive to expose them to as comprehensive a view as possible of the information and arguments that are relevant to the field of study they are pursuing."[28]

After this statement was issued, I received a copy of a complaint against me submitted to the minister of education, the president of the university, and other officials, by members of Im Tirzu. In it, they claimed that I violated the Council's decision because my syllabus was biased. Such letters are not infrequent, and many of my colleagues have also been subjected to complaints such self-appointed "caretakers" of the existing order.

It may be possible for some people to focus on studying mathematics and say nothing as rockets fall twenty kilometers from the campus, but in my classes both Jews and Arabs sought a place to talk about their fear. When the second Intifada erupted, we could hear the gunfire from Issawiyye. Buses were exploding on the way to the campus; people were being killed. Nine students and faculty members were killed in the cafeteria bombing on the Mount Scopus campus, and dozens more were injured. During the second Lebanon war, some students were called up for reserve duty, while Palestinian students feared for their relatives in Lebanon. The wars in Gaza shook the students. There have been hundreds more episodes of violence in Jerusalem over the years, some very near the campus.

To better understand the location of the Mount Scopus campus, I ask you to join me on a tour of the surroundings. We will begin with a walk through the magical botanical gardens towards neighboring Issawiyye—less than ten minutes away.

View of separation wall and Issawiyyeh

Chapter 2

ISSAWIYYE: PALESTINIAN CITIZENS OF ISRAEL (STUDENTS) ENCOUNTER PALESTINIAN YOUTH LIVING UNDER THE OCCUPATION

Could we really not have done more? Wasn't it disheartening that more than half the (9th grade) girls were engaged or soon would be? Had we messed up? Had we done something wrong? Not done enough? [...] Somehow, in the midst of all these feelings, there was still hope. [...] I now understand that something did shift there. [...] Today I see groups of girls who are very aware of themselves, their circumstances, the environment, and society. These are motivated girls, so thirsty for knowledge and skills. They speak about a better future: finishing middle school, high school and perhaps even going to university. "If not us then our daughters" they always say. I see this as change.

—Danya, Campus-Community Student Group Coordinator
in Issawiyye, Personal Diary. Fall, 2010.

Most of the people on campus who come from Issawiyye are cleaners, janitors or cafeteria workers. They don't work for the university, but for private contractors. I think that contract labor is the best metaphor for describing the relationship between the university and Issawiyye: it's a way to get away with not giving the workers their due without being the one to do the exploiting. It's the contractor who is directly responsible for the conditions of employment and the university has no contact with the workers. This is also how the university has handled the blockade of one of the two main roads into the village of Issawiyye for over a decade. It's not the university that has closed the road, they say, but the police who are protecting the university's interests (there's nothing that deters students as much as a tense, political and sometimes violent area). In winter, when we flush the toilets here on Mount Scopus, our sewage floods the streets of Issawiyye. But of course, it's the dilapidated municipal sewage system that's responsible for our shit flowing through Issawiyye; the university has nothing to do with it.

—Uri Agnon, "Looking Down on Issawiyye from the Mount."[1]

The botanical gardens on the campus feature a marvelous array of local and international plants threaded through with narrow, shady paths. A small amphitheater close to the campus boundary affords a panoramic view of the neighboring village of Issawiyye. In the distance, one can see the wall that hems the village in on the west the ever-expanding settlements to the east, and on clear days, the Dead Sea.

The shortest route between the village and the campus has been closed to vehicular traffic since 2002, when a bomb went off in one of the cafeterias, killing nine students and university employees and injuring dozens more. The Mount Scopus campus had already been girded with fences, guards, and security protocols, but after the bombing, its insularity grew even more pronounced. There are four roads into Issawiyye. Two are permanently barricaded and the third—walking distance from student housing (built on land belonging to Issawiyye)—is regularly closed by the police.

As we make our way down toward the village on foot, we can see the ancient carob tree growing at the foot of Mount Scopus. According to Christian tradition, the village of Issawiyye is named after Jesus (Issa in Arabic) who took shelter in the shade of the carob along with his disciples. Muslim tradition cites the tree as a meeting place for the commanders of Salah-A-Din's army, one of whom lent his name, Issa, to the village. Both Muslims and Christians regard this ancient tree as sacred, make pilgrimages of supplication to it.

Tragically, the magnificent tree, adorned with ribbons left by believers, is doomed. It falls within the boundaries of the planned Mount Scopus Slopes National Park, which will devour the last of the lands that might have allowed for the expansion of Issawiyye, along with most of the lands belonging to the Palestinian community of A-Tur. To add insult to injury, the plan refers to the carob tree as an oak. The program's name is ironic but betrays its intentions: "They See Not, Nor Know."[2] An Old Testament reference, the name suggests that the plan was not transparent to the residents of Issawiyye and A-Tur who, unaware, lost most of their remaining development land.

Issawiyye, along with 27 other villages, was conquered in 1967 and annexed to Jerusalem (in contravention of international law). Today it is considered a neighborhood of the "unified" city of Jerusalem. Like most of the city's Palestinian neighborhoods, Issawiyye has gone 20 years with no town planning. The most recent plan was approved by the Jerusalem municipality in 1987 and left inhabitants of the village with almost no land for the construction of new homes. Some of the existing houses were marked as "outside of the area covered by the plan," and therefore "illegal." Since 1967, these Palestinian villagers have been living under occupation—in close proximity to the Hebrew University—forced to build "illegal" homes for their large families because building permits are unattainable. Many of these homes are destined for demolition.

The police and military patrol the village regularly. They mete out collective punishment for village youth throwing stones by setting up frequent roadblocks and stopping every vehicle to check whether the driver has defaulted on city taxes or perhaps radio and television licenses. Sometimes the entire village has its water supply cut off for extended periods.

Despite the physical proximity of Issawiyye to the campus, the village is all but invisible to most Hebrew University students. Not more than a handful of the thousands of students at Hebrew University and Bezalel Art School have set foot in Issawiyye. Not many are aware that 17,000 people are living under occupation in this village, an easy walk from campus. Even fewer know that there are hundreds of children in Issawiyye who sleep in their clothes just in case the bulldozers come to demolish their homes in the middle of the night.

Here and there the village has broken the surface of public consciousness. Samer Issawi,[3] a resident of Issawiyye, was one of the people released from prison in exchange for the release of an Israeli soldier held captive in Gaza. After being arrested for violating the conditions of his release by leaving the Jerusalem municipal area, Issawi went on a 210-day hunger strike. Dozens of Palestinians followed suit in solidarity and there was global media coverage of these protesters willing to die from hunger to assert their right to freedom. Despite worldwide attention, the university saw nothing and said nothing.

In her doctoral dissertation "The Meaning of Home and the Impact of Its Loss on the Palestinian Family in East Jerusalem," Sana Khasheiboun[4] describes how some 100,000 Palestinian residents of East Jerusalem (including the population of Issawiyye) live in fear that their homes, as have others before them, will be demolished. Once issued, demolition orders are sometimes not implemented for years, Khasheiboun explains. Then, without warning, the bulldozers arrive before dawn to raze another home and with it a family's whole world, spirit, and resolve. Selective demolition of homes is a source of the perpetual fear and uncertainty that undermine the social fabric of communities like Issawiyye. Though 39 percent of the residents of Jerusalem are Palestinian, only 13 percent of the city's urban lands are allocated to them for building. According to a municipality estimate, 94 percent of applications for building permits were denied in the year 2007 and some 40 percent of the building that did take place in East Jerusalem was illegal. Issawiyye is one of the most densely populated areas of Jerusalem, with about 20 people per dunam, while the Jerusalem average is 6.5 people per dunam,[5] but the villagers have little, if any, chance of obtaining a building permit.

Life lived in fear of house demolitions also involves serious financial difficulties. Almost 76.4 percent of residents of East Jerusalem and 83.4 percent of Palestinian children in Jerusalem live below the poverty line, as do 36.6 percent of all Jerusalemites and 39.7 percent of Jewish children in the city.[6] In a lecture based on her dissertation, Khsheibun describes the situation thus:

> Selective home demolition is like the slaughtering of lambs—one by one in order to show the others that they may be next. Nobody knows which house will be demolished next, or when, and the community lives in a constant state of fearful anticipation. The International Red Cross provides aid for families whose homes have been demolished in the form of some rice and lentils, a little halva for the children, but the families must find their own alternative accommodation.[7]

Palestinians in Issawiyye have no land rights and no prospect of building new homes. They live with water shortages, lack of shade and greenery, under the constant threat of demolitions, arrest or curfew. There are no sidewalks in Issawiyye and the roads are narrow and winding. There are no trees, no playgrounds, and sewage runs in the streets.

One Small Victory

For a brief moment of respite, let me tell you about one small victory: when a group of Hebrew University faculty members managed to prevent the demolition of Azmi the gardener's home.

Azmi was employed in the aforementioned botanical gardens that connect—and separate—the university and Issawiyye. I met him while taking a course in permaculture there. One day he told me that he'd received a demolition order for the house in which he lived with his wife and five children, on his family's land. I promised to try and help. At one time, years earlier, there had been a small group of students and faculty on campus called Hakampus Lo Yishtok (the campus will not remain silent). Using the membership roster of this now-defunct organization, we approached people to help prevent the demolition of Azmi's home. After two days of correspondence and telephone calls, 53 faculty members sent the mayor a letter calling on him to rescind the demolition order for the home of this man who had been a university employee for over twenty years. The letter was widely published in the press, as was the mayor's decision to suspend the demolition order. This "benefited" Azmi in that the court ruled that his house be "sealed" rather than demolished. Azmi was still forced to leave and it took three long years of legal wrangling before he was able to return home with his family. To this day, more than ten years later, the legal procedures drag on and the threat of demolition still looms.

Despite the exorbitant legal costs, lack of security and perpetual fear, Azmi's family was at least spared the trauma of seeing their home summarily demolished. Azmi was fined 70,000NIS and ordered to "legalize" the house by presenting a detailed plan of the surrounding 15 dunams. The latter was, of course, an impossible demand. Azmi's neighbors, like him, live in fear of having their homes demolished and were too frightened to allow their homes to be surveyed. It would be preposterous to ask residents of a Jewish neighborhood to present a detailed building plan of homes that do not belong to them. Nevertheless, this is something regularly required of residents of east Jerusalem.

Azmi's story, which took but a page to relate here, remains unresolved and subject to the whim of the next judge to find it on his docket. Nevertheless, it does constitute a small victory, attesting to a small group of faculty members who do want to make a difference. Even so, these individuals were not likely to have met Azmi in person or visited his home. They were unlikely to meet with the city official responsible for house demolitions (who made sure I was aware of his younger days in the socialist youth movement and the sleepless nights that afflict him before he orders a house demolished). Nor did they find themselves trying to muster a smile for the municipal attorney who declared he had no intention of intervening to stop the demolition, all the while citing his vacuous plan to demolish an illegal building built by settlers as well. Still, the willingness of some 53 employees of the university to sign a letter to the mayor was something.

Azmi reminds me of the gardener in Andre Brink's *A Dry White Season.*[8] Set in the latter years of apartheid South Africa, the novel describes the upheaval a white family goes through after learning about the fear and constant violence dogging the lives of their gardener's family.

Azmi's house, like all the homes in Issawiyye, is both close to the campus and a million miles away from it. Azmi's was spared because he has worked for the university for many years. What about the anonymous thousands who live in the shadow of the campus, fearing for their homes every day?

Since 2014, soldiers have fired dozens of canisters of tear gas into Issawiyye, sometimes even into homes with children and infants inside them. In some cases, children have needed medical attention. The police use a new type of "sponge" bullet in Issawiyye, one that does a lot of damage. A 16-year-old named Muhammad Sonokrot was reputedly killed by one of these bullets. Two children have lost their sight from them.

With increasing frequency, the police close the last two roads into the village and the Issawiyyens are trapped. Recently, Israeli students and activists from Issawiyye have launched joint protests against these road closures.

In 2015, the university inaugurated the Mandel building, which stands alongside the botanical gardens. The building features a five-story-high glass wall that faces Issawiyye (see photo by Jack Persekian). At a conference convened to discuss campus-Issawiyye relations, my son, Uri Agnon, described the negligible interaction between students and the village and questioned whether the campus sustains any kind of relationship with its immediate surroundings. "Contract labor is the best metaphor for describing the relationship between the university and Issawiyye," he said. "It's a way to get away with not giving the workers their due without being the one to do the exploiting. It's the contractor who is directly responsible for the conditions of employment and the university has no contact with the workers."

The Issawiyye Youth Club

In the winter of 2002, Murad[9] came to see me to discuss starting a youth club for the youth of Issawiyye. He told me that most of the village's children had never seen the sea or even a swimming pool. Like all participants in the Minerva Human Rights Fellows Program, Murad had been asked to select one of 25 Israeli and Palestinian human rights organizations with which to volunteer twice a week throughout the academic year. The list of organizations included those working for women's rights, LGBTQ rights, the rights of Palestinians in the Occupied Territories, those of the Palestinian Arab minority within Israel, people with disabilities, and more.

Murad was one of the few students from East Jerusalem who were accepted—not only to the program but to the university itself. He is married, a father, a graduate student in education. His Hebrew is limited in comparison with that of the Jewish students but also compared to that of Palestinian students from the Galilee and Triangle[10] who learn Hebrew at Israeli schools. Murad was adamant that we had no place discussing the right to education when most of the youth in the nearby village were unable to finish high school. He argued that we should be focusing on the social rights violations happening so close to campus. The lesson in which Murad presented one of the activities he had facilitated with the youth of Issawiyye shook the class, and me, to the core.

Since 2001, the municipality and the education ministry have asserted that there is no room in Jerusalem's schools for thousands of Palestinian children (in response to Supreme Court petitions brought by the Association for Civil Rights and Ir Amim). At the start of the 2016–2017 academic year, there was a shortage of 2,672 classrooms. Fewer Palestinian children attend schools funded by the Israeli authorities than they do private or semiprivate schools, and some 16,700 Palestinian children in Jerusalem are not registered for school at all.[11]

The ongoing shortage of classrooms and the acute lack of resources and personnel have made the probability of obtaining a decent education in East Jerusalem even lower than in Gaza. A study on Palestinian youth in the West Bank, Gaza and Jerusalem found that prospects of participating in cultural activities and attending university are poorer in Jerusalem than they are in the West Bank, and even in Gaza.[12]

As a teacher from East Jerusalem, Murad had managed to corral a group of youth who met twice a week at the community center. This was the only public building in Issawiyye and at the time I was still unaware that it was not heated in the winter, let alone air-conditioned in the summer. In fact, except for some chairs, it had no facilities whatsoever.

In my class, Murad pondered how it might be possible to give youth growing up in a conservative, poor, occupied society a sense that they could have a better future, dream dreams, learn to give and volunteer and experience belonging, fellowship and solidarity.

He shared the following dilemma with his classmates—should he ask each child for 10 shekels ($2.5) to participate in a trip to the seaside? A serious discussion ensued about whether the participants should be asked for "earnest money," as was the norm for the Israeli organization that was sponsoring the trip, or whether this fee should be waived because Murad was concerned that not all the children would be able to get 10 shekels from their parents. Not one of the 14-year-olds in the group had ever seen the sea, though it is less than an hour's drive away.

I vividly recall my sadness at the realization that these children, so nearby, were 10 shekels (some $2.5) away from realizing the dream of visiting the seaside. I was also struck by the absurdity of the situation: a Palestinian from East Jerusalem studying at the Hebrew University, discussing his work with an Israeli organization in the community center of an occupied Palestinian village.

The following year, Ihab took over from Murad. The youth group grew, splitting into three groups of children, none of whom had ever seen the sea or a pool. There is a swimming pool very close to Issawiyye, on the Hebrew University's Mount Scopus campus. We once tried to take the youth group from Issawiyye there. We bought tickets and booked in advance for a group. But as soon as it became clear that the children were from Issawiyye, we were informed that the pool was full. I did not record the conversation, as my colleagues in the law faculty said I should have. Nor did I record a similar conversation I had on a different occasion when a desk attendant at the pool told me that as a university employee I was welcome to buy a membership but that the friend who was with me could only do so if she was a resident of French Hill or married to a diplomat. My Palestinian friend lives in Sheikh Jarrah—walking distance from the pool. For the life of me, I could not fathom why residents of French Hill (the Jewish neighborhood-settlement) were permitted to join, while residents of Issawiyye and Sheikh Jarrah were not. Nor did I understand why a Palestinian married to a diplomat is somehow more acceptable than another Palestinian. However, the university's legal counsel advised me not to question the university's business decisions. It so happens that today, despite the deterrents, the pool on Mount Scopus is now frequented by many Palestinians (though few of them are from Issawiyye). There is not a single public pool in all of East Jerusalem.

But it was not just the pool and the sea that came up in the encounter between my students and the young people from Issawiyye. In class, Ihab spoke of how important and valuable the group was for these deprived youngsters who were mostly confined to overcrowded homes. Other than the group activities, the young people of Issawiyye had no access to social gatherings, recreational spaces, or sources of enrichment outside of school.

One of the dilemmas Ihab presented to the class was whether to accede to parental pressure to offer separate activities on different days for boys and girls. Like most schools in East Jerusalem, and a significant number of Jewish schools in Jerusalem, Issawiyye schools are not co-ed.

Ihab felt that the boys and girls were happy for the chance to meet, even if it was only before and between sessions. These 12–14-year-olds have no other opportunity to interact at all. The school principals, the community center director, and Ihab held two meetings with the parents to establish the ground rules for a program that addressed empowerment, dilemmas, and changes that occur during adolescence, and fostered social involvement. It was eventually agreed that the boys and girls would meet at different times, but not on different days.

My students reported that the boys and girls kept coming back, bringing their friends and younger brothers and sisters. More groups were needed but an expansion of the club's activities would require a larger group of facilitators. The Jerusalemite Palestinian students who ran the club for the first two years were among very few Palestinian students admitted to the Hebrew University.[13] In our search for more Palestinian students/youth facilitators, we approached Perah, the largest volunteer scholarship program in Israel.[14] Approximately 25 percent of Perah mentors are Palestinian citizens of Israel. The organization was pleased to be part of a cooperative program with the neighboring village.

In the summer of 2006, while preparing to expand the program, we organized a meeting at the Issawiyye community center. In attendance were the principals of the two schools (one for girls and one for boys), the Mukhtar (traditional head of the village), the community center director, and past and future student group leaders.

This was my first official meeting in Issawiyye, though the club had already been operational for two years and I had visited Murad and Ihab there. It was there that I met Asuan Zuabi, director of the community center and a graduate student at Hebrew University. Asuan subsequently worked with me for years, as my research and teaching assistant , until her untimely death.

The formal meeting with the principals and the Mukhtar began in Hebrew, out of respect for me. As it proceeded, I requested in my nascent Arabic that the conversation continue in Arabic. Other than myself, all the participants were Palestinian: 10 Palestinian students with Israeli citizenship, and about 10 educators and leaders from the village. Though I understood only part of the conversation, the tension was clear. They spoke of how living in the shadow of the Hebrew University campus had always been a demeaning experience. The first question asked of me was: "Can you stop the University and hospital from dumping their trash in the village?" The Mukhtar wanted to know: "Can you get the road by the university opened so that ambulances can leave without having to weave their way through the village and come out at the only, overcrowded, exit?" "You suggested the opening of a legal clinic. Why did you close it after two years? Why do none of your lawyers defend the boys who get arrested in their homes in the middle of the night?"

The meeting ended with the understanding that there was only so much we could do. It was proposed that we increase the number of groups run by Palestinian students to three for boys and three for girls, offer workshops and legal advice and help foster relations with educators and parents in the village.

Almost all the Palestinian students at the Hebrew University come from outside Jerusalem—mainly from the Galilee and the Triangle. They are among the finest students because the admissions criteria for the university, especially the faculty of law, are extremely high.

The law students who were part of the Minerva group that I facilitated along with the late Aswan Zuabi provided legal aid, gave workshops on the rights of women and children and provided assistance for detained youth. The male students ran the boys' groups and the female students ran the girls' groups. They wondered how to inculcate independence and egalitarianism when the village had no high school for girls. Moreover, some of the girls were not permitted to travel to attend high school elsewhere, and many were married before the age of 17.

The encounter between students who were Palestinian citizens of Israel from the north (Palestinians of '48 as they are known in Arabic) and the people of Issawiyye (Palestinians of '67) was fraught. The former spoke Hebrew, were living independently and studying "with the Jews," and differed from the latter in dialect, language, dress, and appearance. These differences understandably created some complicated dynamics.

It quickly became apparent to me that I could not supervise this group of student volunteers; they needed to process their feelings about their experiences in Issawiyye with experienced Palestinian moderators. Samya Sharkawi facilitated a weekend workshop in Nazareth where the students could share their experience of volunteering with the village youth. These exceptional Palestinian students who had come to Jerusalem to attend the university were confronted with questions about themselves, their identity, and their place in society as they interacted with the youth of Issawiyye. Many of them described the experience as life-changing. That year, 2005–6, there were 60 Human Rights Fellows. The full cohort met once a fortnight and six smaller groups with specific emphases met weekly. One of these groups consisted entirely of Palestinian students volunteering in Issawiyye, the tutor was Palestinian and the lessons were in Arabic. This was initially offensive to some of the Palestinian students. "Are we second-class citizens?" they asked at first. Eventually, as the year progressed, the group became a source of strength for the student volunteers as they dealt with disagreements and painful feelings generated by their experience in Issawiyye. Together they learned how important it was to process the dilemmas that arose, an exercise that benefitted greatly from being held in Arabic with a Palestinian moderator. These sessions were invaluable opportunities to explore and examine their own Palestinian identity in relation to that of Jerusalem Palestinians. At the fortnightly meeting of all 60 students in the program, their group always sat together at the back of the room, but still participated actively in the discussion.

In 2011, the youth club in Issawiyye closed down. A few weeks before the start of the school year, the director of Perah announced that as a result of cutbacks, no scholarships were available. We had no other recourse but to fold. Perhaps the failure was predestined—perhaps a university that stands with its back resolutely turned on the neighboring village is not capable of serving as a conduit to relations between Palestinian citizens of Israel and Jerusalem Palestinians living under occupation. Perah closed down the program because all the group volunteer programs had been cut and that the only scholarships remaining were for personal mentors. The truth is that Perah did not withdraw from the long-term plan because the project was unsuccessful, but because it was too successful. Every year, the majority of students who applied to Perah for scholarships in Jerusalem elected to volunteer as youth group leaders in

Issawiyye. While the change in the village might have been negligible, the students who engaged with the village's youth and tried to build a future with them were very much affected. The biggest, most formative change that they reported at the end of the year was not in Issawiyye, but in themselves.

The theoretical background to our group work in Issawiyye was Paulo Freire's *Pedagogy of the Oppressed*, according to which educational processes are never neutral. They require action and reflection on that action. The social contexts of inequality are essential to understanding learning, which is a political process. By contrast, Perah's mentorship model is based on the relationship between one student and one child and disengaged from the sociopolitical context. Freire suggests that it is essential for students to associate knowledge with working toward social change on the local level and beyond.[15] Perah purports to be an apolitical organization that emphasizes personal volunteerism and mentoring, but ultimately all it does is provide children with a pleasant, superficial, experience that poses no threat to the existing social order.

Interacting with the youth from the village strengthened the sense of common identity for the students who were Palestinian citizens of Israel. Perah as an organization could not facilitate this interaction because its individual mentoring programs did not interface with the identity issues that the students were dealing with.

For over forty years, the vast majority of scholarships awarded in Israel have been for personal mentoring, and every time Perah is required to cut its budget the group programs are the first to go—even though they are the ones that interest students the most and have the most long-term impact.[16] Perah's leadership is clear on this matter: the organization's central focus is personal mentoring. Group work, unlike personal work, raises questions of identity, nationalism, and belonging—political questions that are noticeably absent from the discourse of Perah and the campus as a whole.

Palestinian Students in Israeli Academia

The ongoing Israeli–Palestinian conflict has resulted in totally disparate experiences for Jewish and Arab students in Israel's colleges and universities. Jewish students belong to the majority; Palestinian Arab students belong to the minority that remained within Israel's borders after most of its community was uprooted during the 1948 Nakba.[17] Inequality and socioeconomic gaps between Jews and Palestinians in Israel are multidimensional, deep, ongoing and usually institutionalized. Discrimination and inequality occur across a broad array of fields, including employment, income, housing, planning, and building laws, infrastructure and development, health, welfare, and education.[18]

Over the last seven years, the Israel Council of Higher Education has invested millions of shekels in plans to increase the number of Arab students. Indeed, after a rise of 80 percent in their numbers, in the 2016–17 academic year, 16 percent of undergraduate students, 13 percent of graduate students, and 6.3 percent of doctoral candidates in Israeli institutions of higher education were Palestinian.[19] Palestinian students in Israel have very few Arab faculty members to look to as role models; Arabs account for only 2.6 percent of faculty and 1.5 percent of administrative staff in Israeli universities. This is the case on Mount Scopus as well. The Hebrew University has 920 faculty members, only 20 of whom (2 percent) are Arabs. Representation is even lower in the administrative faculty, with fewer than 20 Arabs among the 1850 employees.[20]

Most Palestinian citizens of Israel prefer to study in the Occupied Territories or Jordan. Those who do attend Israeli universities report feelings of alienation and isolation, difficulty coping with the Hebrew, and fear of compromising their Arabic. In most Israeli institutions, lectures are held on Christian and Muslim holidays and Palestinian students need special permission to miss class on these occasions.[21] Moreover, Palestinian students in Israel—where there is not a single Arabic-medium university—also face restrictions with regard to their use of Arabic. For all these reasons, Palestinian citizens of Israel are more likely to pursue academic studies in other countries than in Israel.

In *Inequality in Education*,[22] I invoke different feminist theories to elucidate how Arab students in the Israeli education system are discriminated against. The development of feminist thought is commonly divided into three waves. Each wave features a different perspective on the question of equality between men and women, from the struggle for formal equal rights to the struggle for representation of the distinct voices and experiences of women in dominant social spheres to the demand that a diversity of voices be heard and that the struggles of various groups of women be acknowledged. Inequality in the Israeli education system can be seen as analogous.

First Wave: Discriminatory Resource Allocation

First-wave feminists focused on questions of representation and accessibility. To expose inequality between women and men in society, they asked questions that might be characterized as "quantitative": how much women earned in comparison with men, how many women were in positions of influence and power in society, and so on. These questions concern formal aspects of equality, the assumption being that as more women occupy positions of power, the status and welfare of women will improve. The objective of this type of feminism was equality between men and women in salary, roles, opportunities, representation, and access to positions of influence. In the Israeli context, this would mean that the more women are elected to the Knesset, hold key positions in the Education Ministry or major corporations, and perform visible tasks, the more equitable society will be. Borrowing from the feminist perspective, if we wish to understand inequality in the Arab education system we must begin with a quantitative question: how much does the Ministry of Education invest in the Arab education system in comparison with the Jewish–Israeli education system?[23]

Only 34 percent of Arab high school students graduate with a baccalaureate, and even less meet the admissions requirements for Israeli institutions of higher education. This is a function of long-term and multifaceted discrimination against Arab education in Israel. Governmental investment in the Arab education system is significantly lower than in the Jewish–Israeli education system,[24] with the former getting fewer supervision and training hours, less funding for special programs, art, field trips, sciences, and informal education. As a rule, Arab schools' physical facilities are more rundown, and the amount of money invested in an Arab student is, on average, one-fifth of the investment in a Jewish student. According to Ministry of Education data, the state invested in 2018 an average of 40,000 NIS per year on a student in the state religious high school, 31,000 NIS on a student in the Hebrew state high school, and 24,000 NIS on a student in Arab Israeli high school. But discrimination against Arab children in the Israeli education system is manifest in more than just financial resources.

The few Arab students that meet Israeli higher education's admissions criteria must also take the psychometric exam. This standardized test discriminates against Arab test-takers: Jewish students consistently score an average of 100 points higher than Arab students and have done so for years. Tests are developed by the Israel National Institute for Testing and Evaluation, which also translates the exams from Hebrew into Arabic. The Institute and the Education Ministry have known about this discrimination for years, but too little is being done to change the situation. The exam also discriminates against women: they score an average of 41 points less than men.[25]

Second Wave: Discrimination against Arab Educational Leadership

Second-wave feminists argued that equality between men and women should not require that women emulate men or become a part of the male world. Instead, they argued, society should recognize the unique contributions of women and accord them equal value. This iteration of feminism began asking what I call "how" questions: How are categories such as "feminine" and "masculine" constructed as part of a patriarchal structure? How are women's voices and experiences marginalized from society's dominant discourses? How would these discourses look different if a feminine voice were integrated into them? Professor Carol Gilligan of Harvard University published the now-classic book *In a Different Voice* in the 1980s.[26] This momentous work challenged the accepted hierarchy in psychology and culture that positioned feminine behavior as morally inferior to masculine behavior. Gilligan argues that there is an underlying interpretive problem with judging one as inferior to the other, that men and women actually hold different conceptions of morality and justice that cannot be placed on the same scale, and that conventional ranking of moral systems is determined solely by masculine categories and thought processes.

Gilligan demonstrates this by analyzing Kohlberg's theory of the stages of moral development.[27] Kohlberg's research focused on how two children, Jack and Amy, dealt with a hypothetical moral dilemma—what should a person do if his wife is ill and requires medicine that can be obtained at a local pharmacy but is too expensive for him to buy? Kohlberg consistently ranked Amy's answers as less morally developed than Jack's, while describing Jack as having a more balanced and sophisticated approach to justice. Whereas Jack engaged in a logical abstraction of the situation and considered the interests of the man caring for his wife and the property rights of the pharmacist, Amy tried to arrive at a solution that would connect them based on a sense of responsibility and concern, a connection that would bridge the apparent gap between the two parties' interests. Gilligan argues that the error is not in Amy's thought process but in the researchers' interpretation. What Kohlberg's study described as a logical fallacy and an absence of independent thought, Gilligan views as an alternative means of conflict resolution founded on an understanding of the web of human relationships involved—on empathy and communication. Amy's approach was neither underdeveloped nor immature relative to Jack's; it is Kohlberg's method that was blind to the assumptions under which it was operating.

In light of this conclusion, Gilligan calls for breaking with assumptions that allow only one voice to be heard and that organize society around uniform notions. She asks, why the feminine voice is not heard and argues that society would benefit from authentic dialogue between different voices and from a mixture of logic and empathy.

Borrowing from this perspective, I ask the following question: How would the Israeli education system benefit from equal representation of Arab leaders? This question is a departure from quantitative questions such as those raised by the first wave of feminists. Instead, it gives voice to other key questions, including: How does the scant representation of Arab educators in influential positions in the Israeli education system impact representation of the specific interests of Arab teachers and students in Israel? How does their absence from these positions undermine the possibility of creating an education system capable of realizing the autonomous culture and educational ambitions of Israel's Arab citizens?

For decades, the appointment of Arab teachers and school principals has been contingent on approval from the General Security Service (or "Shabak"). Arab educators have no say in the Israeli Ministry of Education's planning, decision- or policy-making. Arabs are grossly underrepresented in the ministry. There is not a single Arab district supervisor or administrator. The Israeli education system declares that it strives to inculcate democratic values, human rights, and active citizenship, but these values are not evident in its practices. Many Arab educators argue that equal representation for Arabs in key ministry administrative positions would only be possible if an autonomous Arab educational administration were established. In a spirit akin to second-wave feminism, they argue that ensuring equal representation of the Arab minority in the Ministry of Education is only a necessary first step. Safeguarding the specific interests and characteristics of the Arab education system requires an autonomous Arab educational administration (much like the administration of the Jewish–Israeli state-religious education system) the role of which would be to appoint personnel, determine priorities, educational goals and curricula, and plan, implement, oversee and evaluate its activities. Like the call to make space for the marginalized feminine voice, experience, and characteristics, the Arab educators' call to establish an autonomous Arab educational administration is an attempt to claim space in the Israeli educational landscape, to occupy an equal position, with the basic freedom and necessary resources to shape its own trajectory.

Third Wave: Discrimination in Educational Curricula

Inequality in education is not merely the result of inequitable distribution of resources and representational inequality in planning, administrative and supervisory positions in the education system, and also of inequality in the curricula being taught. Third-wave feminists brought up the importance of multiculturalism and the honoring of diverse voices. In the United States, it was black women writing about class and identity who contributed to the feminist discussion; in Israel, it was Mizrahi and Palestinian women who added their voices to the debate. This wave of feminists argued that their socioeconomic status and cultural origins impacted how they were perceived and that creating an equitable and just society would only be possible if a diversity of voices were heard. Women like bell hooks linked color, class, and gender, challenging the notion of sisterhood among all women by asking whether white women faced with "the glass ceiling" are in comparable positions to women living in poverty and struggling with "the sticky floor." Third-wave feminism also refers to the contribution of queer theory, which added gender diversity to the range of voices worthy of being heard and undermined the essentialist dichotomy between women and men. Third-wave feminism taught us that an equitable society is possible only if the voices of marginalized groups are included. I apply the same principle when I ask: What materials are studied in Israeli schools?

Tremendous efforts have been made to prevent Arab schools from teaching about Palestinian culture, history, and literature. For example, the Arab education system in Israel uses a significant amount of material that is translated from and does not reflect the students' cultural world. Palestinian cultural capital is sidelined, at best. Ismael Abu Saad writes the following about Arab Israeli schools:

> The state educational system in Israel functions effectively to maintain the cultural, socioeconomic, and political subordination of Israel's Palestinian Arab citizens through the imposition of aims, goals, and curricula to which the students cannot relate, and the substandard and discriminatory provision of educational resources, programs, and services; all of which result in markedly poorer levels of educational achievement and lower rates of students qualified to enter higher education. As with every other aspect of the education system in Israel, these inequitable outcomes are not a matter of chance, but rather a matter of policy; the racially derogatory attitudes towards the Palestinian Arab minority in Israel have been translated into discriminatory practices in the state-run educational system. Thus, these practices have placed Palestinian Arabs on an unequal footing with regard to their social, economic and political development vis-à-vis the Israeli Jewish majority, and have led to the institutionalization of an education system that perpetuates racist attitudes and practices.

Another dimension of inequity in education is language. Students learn to express themselves through academic writing. In the case of Israeli universities, this means writing in Hebrew and while acquisition of the language may increase Palestinian students' chances of finding employment in Israel, it distances them from reading, writing, and proficiency in Classical Arabic. Many Palestinian students describe fierce competition with their Hebrew-speaking peers and others fear losing their mastery of the Arabic language.[28]

View from Redeemer Church tower

Double Alienation: Students Who Are Palestinian Citizens of Israel Living in Jerusalem

In Jerusalem, the city of borders and sharp contradictions, we, the Arab students attending Hebrew University—a university built right on the border, the border of Israeli power in 1948—would carry out the typical and familiar ceremonies: lazy visits to the Old City's alleys, sitting around on the steps of Bab Al-Amud. And there were the disturbing sights of Border Police officers harassing Palestinian women selling parsley and mint "without a permit" at the market entrance. And there were the soldiers' repeated shouts demanding that the local youth show them their identity cards (Identity. To this day, it is not clear to me who is really the one with the identity problem). Jerusalem swept us away with the smells of its marketplaces and the faces of the female tourists visiting from all over the world. The restaurants, the array of newspapers on the stands, the theater—all of it drew in. We were enchanted. And it would always play the part of the seductive, hard-to-get city. But it's hard-to-get disposition did not stop us from constantly trying to be a part of it, to become the other that has become a part of us.

Jerusalem was my first encounter with the "city," with an open urban space, and with the "self." It was my first real encounter with nationalism and modernism. But my first city was an occupied one. Raif Zreik, *The Way Back*[29]

Some 13 percent of Hebrew University students are Palestinian citizens of Israel, most of them female. Two characteristics distinguish them from the rest of the Palestinian students in Israeli academia: First, because the university is far away from Arab towns (and also because residents of East Jerusalem have difficulty getting accepted to university) most of them are Israeli citizens from the Galilee and Triangle. They live in the dorms, far from their homes and families. Second, their alienation extends beyond the campus to East Jerusalem, where they are conscious of the differences between them and Jerusalemite Palestinians.

In her MA thesis, Yaara Saadi studied the experiences of Palestinian students on the Mount Scopus campus of the Hebrew University. The students she interviewed felt foreign: "like visitors who leave no trace,"[30] Saadi notes that these feelings of foreignness dominated the students' experiences on campus, and in general. She describes physical segregation on campus, with Palestinian students tending to gather in the Forum (the hub of the campus) and sitting apart from Jewish students in class, sticking together and not participating much in discussions. She illustrates how the gathering of Arab students in the Forum, at the heart of the campus, simultaneously marginalizes them and places them at the center of the space in which they feel so foreign.

Over the years, many Palestinian students have told me that they never once uttered a word in class during their entire time at the university. In a meeting of Minerva Human Rights Fellows graduates in October 2012, Fatma spoke of the tensions and sense of confusion that Palestinian students experienced during the second Intifada, and how she and other Palestinian students preferred not to attend classes. The Minerva class was the only place in which they felt safe to express themselves.

> In other places, other courses, I could not have said a single word; I think that no lecturer was interested in what I thought, [I felt] as if I did not exist. Everyone knew that there were a few Arabs [in the class] but there was no interest in hearing us.

Both male and female students in Saadi's study reported this sense of alienation. One male student explained: "The Palestinian students, myself included, sit together in class—usually in the back row. We feel detached from the lecturers; they don't call on us, and we are listening to things meant for other ears."[31]

Rabah Halabi describes the Palestinian students at the Hebrew University's feeling that they are "absent presences," focusing on their language difficulties, and other difficulties that cause alienation, frustration, and even rage.[32]

Jerusalemite Palestinians and Palestinian citizens of Israel spoke a lot about the difficulties inherent in the encounter between them, which extend beyond the campus. The latter said they did not feel they belonged in the city because the Jerusalemite Palestinians perceived them as too much like the Jews (silver-spoon Arabs is what they are called in East Jerusalem and elsewhere in the Occupied Territories).

Two female Palestinian students, volunteers at the SAWA center in East Jerusalem and workshop facilitators in East Jerusalem schools, shared how difficult it was to discuss sexuality with girls who are so sheltered from it. They wondered whether the workshops might give rise to unnecessary anxiety. The volunteers described a middle school class that was held in the living room of a house that held three other classrooms. They said that the schoolgirls were afraid to speak. I asked whether the schoolgirls' wariness had anything to do with the facilitators being from the north, or '48 Palestinians (citizens of Israel), rather than from Jerusalem. I touched a nerve. A student named Abir answered, "Yes. You know what they think of us here, the Jerusalem

Palestinians. Those of us who live in the dorms are thought of as promiscuous and the more traditional Palestinian society in Jerusalem sees us as a threat to their daughters' morals." I asked how the schoolgirls knew that the students were not from Jerusalem. The second student, Rula, explained that the way she wears her hijab makes her instantly identifiable as a '48 Palestinian. "In Jerusalem, they wear the hijab differently," she explained. The other students, all from the north, added that there are also certain linguistic differences, including usage of occasional Hebrew words, which is unacceptable to Jerusalem Palestinians. Most also noted that their dress style is often different from that of the Jerusalem Palestinians.

These intra-Palestinian differences aroused much curiosity among the Jewish students. "I'd like to ask a question, even though it might be inappropriate," said Ruth. "Do you date Jerusalem Palestinians?" The discussion turned to defining exactly what "dating" means. Rula, the same student who described her difficult encounters with Jerusalem Palestinian schoolgirls, explained that if she were to marry a Jerusalem Palestinian, she might encounter bureaucratic problems as he would not have Israeli citizenship, and if they have children, and the Jerusalem father is unlucky enough to live on the wrong side of the separation wall, their children might not be registered at all. "Why don't we know these things about East Jerusalem?" asked Yael as the lesson came to an end. "How is it possible that none of us knew what was happening so close to us?" Hila, another student, approached me after the lesson and confessed, "I knew about everything you said about the identity documents of Israeli Palestinians and Jerusalem Palestinians because I work in airport security. I knew there were different documents and that we handled them differently, but until today I never considered the impact of those differences on Palestinians."

View from Sheikh Jarrah

Chapter 3

SHEIKH JARRAH: QUEER THEORY AND THE NATURE OF LAW

I begin the Minerva Human Rights Fellows course by asking the students to share stories of injustice—something they experienced that day, the day before, or as children; a time when they felt something was wrong or unfair. Their stories usually provide the basis for defining human rights discourse, which pertains to interactions between individuals/groups and the state and authorities. It is also a good way to introduce the students to one another. Every year, at least one of the Palestinian students describes being prevented from entering the campus by security guards, or stopped in the street by the police "because I look Arab." Every year at least one Jewish student speaks about discrimination in the army—"I felt that I deserved to go to officer training, but they wouldn't let me."

Some of the stories make a long-lasting, even indelible, impression. Sitting in a circle, we take turns sharing. Usually, no one interrupts. I try to encourage the students to just listen. But on one occasion, Salwa was speaking about her past and a woman named Reut, who was sitting across from her, was so shocked that she questioned the veracity of the story. "You're saying that you were accepted into medical school but you can't go because you are from East Jerusalem?" she asked. I myself hadn't known that Palestinian East Jerusalemites were not allowed to study medicine at the university, though I had heard terrible stories about the difficulties encountered by East Jerusalem students. I wanted to let Salwa continue talking about how she was finishing a degree in occupational therapy and was happy with this choice. But Reut decided to investigate. Her inquiry confirmed that indeed, because Salwa lived in the "Jordanian" or Palestinian section of Beit Safafa, she was prohibited from studying medicine. Reut suggested that the class organize to advocate for the right of East Jerusalem students to study medicine at the Hebrew University and stop this from happening again. Two years later, there was a medical student from East Jerusalem in my class.

In 2009, a student named Ido told us about a summer he and his friends had spent in Sheikh Jarrah, a neighborhood near campus, trying to protect

Palestinian families from being evicted from their homes by the police so that Jewish settlers could live in them. He spoke about the neighborhood, but also about the experiences that he and other transgender activists had while trying to protect the families.

> We came to stay over in the neighborhood before the eviction, as Israeli and international activists had been doing every night. Because the family was traditional, men and women had separate sleeping arrangements. About a quarter-hour after it became clear that we intended to sleep together, the international activists informed us that we could not sleep in the house because we "were not trusted." With all due understanding to traditional Palestinian families who were uncomfortable with our gender presentation, I remember my own feelings of discomfort.

Ido introduced himself to the class at the beginning of the year and addressed the complexity of Israeli Palestinian conflict in Jerusalem. He explained the problem with integrating the two struggles in which he was invested: the struggle against the eviction of Palestinian families from their home in Sheikh Jarrah and the struggle against ostracism of him and his queer friends, in both Israeli and Palestinian society. He also spoke about the sex reassignment he had been undergoing for the past year.

Ido always sat next to me. I had met him two years earlier when he was still called Hadas and on two occasions I addressed him with feminine pronouns and apologized. He smiled and told me not to worry, that the subversion of the male/female dichotomy was exactly what was interesting and challenging. Thanks to Ido, the group got to discuss the intersection of causes, societal tolerance of differences, and dilemmas between Israeli activists and Palestinians. With his assistance, I began to apply queer theory to understanding the legal realities prevailing in Jerusalem.

Sheikh Jarrah, Jerusalem

The neighborhood of Sheikh Jarrah in East Jerusalem stretches from the Old City to Mount Scopus. It has shady streets lined with magnificent old mansions. Many senior foreign employees of the UN and NGOs live in upper Sheikh Jarrah, which is also home to several consulates. St. John of Jerusalem Eye Hospital is tucked into one of the streets near the grand Ambassador Hotel atop the hill.[1] Further down is the gorgeous American Colony Hotel. Between them, in the wadi, a little bit below the grocery store that never closes and the produce stand that is famous throughout the city is the tomb of Shimon Hatzadik—Simon the Just. Beside that is a modest compound of single-story homes, coveted by Jewish settlers, that has been the heart of a bitter struggle for years. Before 1948, Jews and Arabs coexisted peacefully in Sheikh Jarrah.

In 1956, 28 Palestinian refugee families who had lost their homes and lands in the 1948 Nakba were given building plots in Sheikh Jarrah by an UNRWA (UN Relief and Works Agency for Palestinian Refugees in the Near East) lottery. In exchange for these homes, the families relinquished their UN refugee documents and the accompanying rights. After the conquest of East Jerusalem in 1967, two Jewish settler organizations petitioned the court, claiming that the land these homes had been built on had belonged to them before 1948. They demanded that the Palestinian residents pay rent or be evicted. The 28 refugee families are prevented by law from returning to the homes they had possessed before 1948 in Haifa, Jaffa, and Sarafand—areas which are now in Israel. Nevertheless, the courts affirmed the Jewish organization's petition to seize possession of the Palestinian family homes that had been built on privately owned land. All 28 Palestinian families received eviction notices. Four families were evicted and their homes occupied by Jewish settlers. The court also ruled that a fifth family, the Al Kurd family had built an illegal extension to their home. Policemen evicted the family from the ostensibly illegal room, which is now occupied by Jewish settlers and a dog.

The story of how the Palestinians of Sheikh Jarrah—refugees who lost their homes once before, in 1948, and who live in fear for their homes still— illustrates the problematic nature of the Israeli law, specifically the Absentees Property Law, which perpetuates inequality and discrimination against Arabs in Israel.

Addressing a university conference, Justice Emeritus Michael Ben Yair— Israel state attorney general from 1993 to 1996—spoke about his childhood in the neighborhood of Sheikh Jarrah, also known as the Georges neighborhood.[2] He described how Jewish residents were forced to leave their homes in 1948 and given apartments or homes abandoned by Palestinians in West Jerusalem.

> We were given two apartments and a store in Sheikh Bader in exchange for our assets in Sheikh Jarrah. We were not the only ones who were given alternative housing that had belonged to Arabs who had fled. All residents of the Sheikh Jarrah/Shimon Hatzadik neighborhood were given alternative housing in property abandoned by Arabs who fled to East Jerusalem. [...] One could say with relative certainty that the number of properties abandoned in west Jerusalem was much higher than the number abandoned in east Jerusalem. They were also, in all likelihood, worth more then, and they certainly are today.[3]

The Absentees Property Law is comprised of three different laws, each of which applies to different populations. The first (Absentees Property Law, 1950) gives control over the property of Arab residents who fled the state of Israel to the Custodian of Absentee Property. By law, the custodian can release the property to its historical owners, though such a return of property to Palestinians has never occurred. Instead, the custodian has transferred properties to the Lands Authority, sold them, or allowed their appropriation for Jewish public use. This law is responsible for the transfer of the vast majority of houses and lands left by their Arab owners in 1948.

The second, the Law and Administration Ordinance (1970), applies only to the homes of Jews who fled East Jerusalem for West Jerusalem or other places in the country. According to this law, the custodian is required to release the property to anyone who can prove historical ownership from the period before the 1948 war. Based on the Law and Administration Ordinance, the Sephardic Council, which had owned the open field beside the tomb in Sheikh Jarrah, demanded the return of the property on the basis of historical ownership.

The third law applies to Palestinians who became residents of Israel after 1967, that is, residents of East Jerusalem, which was annexed to Israel in 1967. According to this law, these people are not permitted to reclaim their pre-1948 properties, even if they can prove ownership. They can only apply for monetary compensation, which is always much lower than the current value of the property.

To put it bluntly, as Alon Harel points out, the laws of ownership are ethnicity-based. Jewish owners of property abandoned in East Jerusalem can reclaim ownership (even if they were fully compensated in the form of Palestinian properties in Israel). Palestinians who lost property in West Jerusalem are not entitled to reclaim their property. At best they can demand (inadequate) compensation. Palestinians who are not residents of Israel are not entitled to any claim or compensation at all.[4]

This legislation provided legal channels through which Jews could obtain monetary compensation for properties abandoned in East Jerusalem even if they received substitute properties in West Jerusalem. With regard to the Palestinians, not only is there no legal way to have their property in West Jerusalem released, but they are vulnerable to eviction from their current homes in East Jerusalem if Jews can prove historical ownership of them. This is what happened in Sheikh Jarrah.

Such discriminatory law in Jerusalem undermines and challenges the binary division between citizens and non-citizens of Israel that Israel has proffered since 1967. It is generally believed that Israeli citizens live in a democracy with full civil rights, while the Palestinians in the Occupied Territories live under "temporary" military occupation without civil rights. The story of Sheikh Jarrah and the Absentee Property Law compels us to question whether this dichotomy between civil rights and democracy on one side of the Green Line (which has been erased from the maps) and the lack of rights on the other side is even possible. The broader question pertains to the nature of law.

Common perception is that the law encompasses and protects the social values held by the members of a society. The legitimation of law is contingent on these values being common to all. Due process, civil rights, legality, equality under the law, freedom of expression and the right to privacy—all the liberal values of the rule of law—are perceived as relevant to wider society in addition to being descriptors of how the justice system operates.

In contrast to the classic liberal understanding of the law, there are sociological perspectives that view the law in terms of "conflict" or "coercion" in the interests of the ruling class. Marxist theory is known for emphasizing the coercive capacity of the law, but liberal thinkers have also developed complex positions that go beyond seeing the law as social consensus. Advocates of Critical Legal Studies (CLS) propose that the law is not just a consensual reflection of liberal values, nor merely a coercive instrument of the ruling class. But the law is fraught with more possibilities, contradictions, and tensions, either model accounts for. The law can be a source of control and protection, and simultaneously constitute a defense, a resource both for those with power and those without.

Most legal professionals and academics in Israel hold a liberal view of the country, seeing it as a democracy in which the law reflects social norms. Their position is, however, compromised by the fact that this model of legal liberalism does not apply in the Occupied Territories. There, military rule deprives the Palestinian residents of basic civil rights. The "law" works through a system of military orders designed to serve the interests of the occupier and regulate, govern, and control the lives of the occupied.

How can Israeli liberals, especially lawyers who are witness to this dual legal system that differentiates between the territories (Palestinians) and Israelis, resolve this anomaly? Stanley Cohen called the technique employed to do this "geographical magic": "In Israel itself, they claim' everything is okay, but 'over there,' across the Green Line, there is a military government, there is no rule of law, there are no civil rights, no human rights. Everyone understands this and nothing can be done about it until there is a political solution." Cohen wrote that he found it "astonishing that anyone can seriously take this illusion to be reality [...]. The illusion that there is a boundary that marks the Occupation as a separate social territory-prevents full comprehension of how the norms of legality applied 'over there' spread into, penetrate and contaminate every element of the legal system in Israel itself".[5]

The law school

Since the occupation of the territories in 1967, the state of Israel has maintained a dual justice system: for the Palestinians living under occupation, military courts with Israeli prosecutors, lawyers, and judges in military uniform; for Israeli citizens, including those living in settlements in the Occupied Territories, a separate system of civil courts.

Invoking queer theory, we might regard the matter of Sheikh Jarrah and the Palestinian residents of East Jerusalem as a challenge to the binary distinction between the Occupied Territories and "democratic Israel." Queer theory, which emerged in the 1990s, explains how any behavior that doesn't fit into the binary categories of male and female is perceived as aberrant and socially unacceptable. Because dichotomous-gendered thinking is deeply rooted in our cultures, encountering a "woman" who looks like a "man," or a person who challenges the boundary between "male" and "female," undermines and challenges social consensus. Judith Butler, one of the most important voices in queer theory, claims that the received discourse surrounding gender and sexuality presumes an internal ontological existence of gender—a sort of gendered nucleus with which we humans are born. Butler argues that this genderization is created by language, attire, and behavior—what she refers to as performative acts. She explains how we mimic idealized models that are constructed outside of our existence. These determine the prescribed appearance and demeanor of a "man" or "woman." This system of rules is so powerful that we perpetuate it continually.[6]

Borrowing from queer theory, I suggest that the Palestinians in Jerusalem constitute a challenge to the legal definitions that categorize people and police their identities as "Israelis" or "Palestinians." Not entitled to the same rights as Jews, Jerusalem's Palestinians are in a type of civil purgatory: they are neither citizens of Israel nor Palestinians from the Occupied Territories. Jerusalem's Palestinians challenge the illogical division accepted by most Israelis, which portrays Israeli law and military law in the Occupied Territories as completely separate. Territorially, Palestinians who live in Jerusalem fall under Israeli law, but they are not citizens of Israel and their rights as residents of Jerusalem can be taken away from them. Jerusalem's Palestinians must constantly perform their connection with the city and prove that it is the anchor of their lives to avoid losing their blue identity cards, which are their ticket to remaining in their own homes. Proving this connection to the city is an arduous and intrusive procedure. A plethora of documentation, including the deed to an apartment or rental contract, all bills with the petitioner's name on them, confirmations that all the family's children are enrolled in Jerusalem schools, health fund confirmations, salary slips or unemployment documentation, subsidies, bank accounts and more. Tens of thousands of residents have lost their blue identity cards because they left the city for over two years to study, for work reasons, because they hold a foreign passport, or because they failed in some other way to prove that "municipal Jerusalem is the center of their lives." Tens of thousands of Palestinians lost their status as Jerusalemites after the building of the separation wall put their neighborhoods outside of the (arbitrarily determined) city limits.

Since the 1990s, Israel has engaged in what human rights organizations call the "silent transfer," which sets up many different bureaucratic obstacles in order to force Palestinians out of Jerusalem. Declared Israeli policy as it appears in the vision plan is to maintain a 70 percent Jewish presence in Jerusalem. This policy, which makes no sense demographically or practically, employs various means to ensure that Jerusalem, which today is about 40 percent Palestinian, will have a Jewish majority. This silent transfer policy, combined with the bureaucratic difficulties heaped on Palestinians in Jerusalem, aims to encourage them to leave the city because they have little chance of obtaining building permits, have high rates and fines imposed on them, do not have enough classrooms, or employment opportunities. Nevertheless, they prefer to remain in Jerusalem and fight for their rights as residents of the city.

Sumud is the Palestinian response to discriminatory Israeli policy in Jerusalem. The vast majority of Jerusalemite Palestinians prefer to remain in the city despite the difficulties they face. Sumud—steadfast adherence to the land despite difficulties—is a nonviolent political ideology embraced by Palestinians who refuse to give in to Israel's not-so-subtle pressure and leave their homes.

Raja Shehadeh explains that there are three ways to resist the occupation: blind hatred, silent submission, and Sumud.

> You samid, choose to stay in that prison, because it is your home, and because you fear that if you leave, your jailer will not allow you to return. Living like this, you must constantly resist the twin temptations of either acquiescing in the jailer's plan in numb despair, or becoming crazed by consuming hatred for your jailer and yourself, the prisoner.[7]

The separation wall that cuts certain Palestinian neighborhoods off from others in Jerusalem, bearing no relation to the Green Line, was meant to reduce the number of Palestinians in Jerusalem. However, many Palestinians who suddenly found themselves outside the city limits rented apartments in the city to avoid losing their permanent residence status. The price of apartments in East Jerusalem is high because of the demand resulting from Palestinians moving to Jewish neighborhoods.

The Jerusalem Palestinians choose Sumud as a strategic practice of remaining on the land, in patience and faith that the difficulties will not unseat confidence in their rights to the land. The residents of Sheikh Jarrah, whose homes and lands were left in 1948 and are now occupied by Jews, don't want to repeat this cycle. They choose Sumud.

The Sheikh Jarrah Solidarity

The Sheikh Jarrah Solidarity group was comprised largely of Israeli students and faculty members, but the protest hardly reached the campus. The Israeli struggle began with marches from West Jerusalem to Sheikh Jarrah and developed into a weekly protest in the neighborhood itself. Protesters gathered outside evacuated homes along with the evicted families and Palestinian protesters.

In addition to students and faculty members, members of the LGBTQ community were prominent in these demonstrations. The police arrested dozens of protesters every week, many of them students. It happened that on Hanukah in 2009, the Jerusalem police arrested fifty Israeli drummers and clowns who were marching from West Jerusalem to Sheikh Jarrah, singing samba rhythms. They brought energy to the demonstration with their antics and colorful clothing, painting a strong contrast to the soldiers. The arrests continued to happen every week and many international activists joined the Israeli and Palestinian demonstrators. In October 2010, the demonstration was attended by former president of the United States, Jimmy Carter; the former president of Ireland, Mary Robinson; and the Indian activist Hala bahta.

In September 2011, the Israeli organizers of Sheikh Jarrah Solidarity announced, without consulting the residents of the neighborhood or the activists, that the weekly demonstrations would be ending. Despite this decision, the demonstrations are still happening today, organized by neighborhood residents along with Israeli activists. The leaders of Solidarity decided to establish an independent think-tank and research institute devoted to a reconceptualization of all aspects of public life in Israel, called Molad. The aim of this center as presented on the website is "to inform public debate with responsible content that meets the highest possible standards of research and analysis—the dearth of which has played a crucial role in Israel's ongoing state of crisis."[8]

The sudden suspension of the demonstrations and creation of an "independent and non-partisan" research organization, instead, damaged the most significant protest movement at work in Jerusalem at the time. The institutionalization of protest through the establishment of internationally funded organizations in both Israel and Palestine is a practice that has become prevalent in the past 20 years. But no matter how much these organizations try to assume professional establishment status and avoid political affiliation, they are, ultimately, considered left-wing. (Molad was originally funded by the New

Israel Fund but later dissociated from the NIF because it is too closely tied to the left.) The establishment of such research centers not only undermines the protest movement, but it also signifies relinquishing the idea of the academy as a space for research and critical discussion. The solution offered by Molad to "Israel's ongoing state of crisis," which it believes to be the result, among other things, of a lack of "research and analysis," is to establish a research center outside of the academy rather than challenge the academy to research and work toward changing the current reality.

In terms borrowed from Bourdieu, the members of Sheikh Jarrah Solidarity leveraged their status as academic researchers but elected to distance their research activities from their academic undertakings. Molad thus perpetuated and exacerbated the rift maintained by Israeli academics between their off-campus political activism and research, and the ostensible objective neutrality of their on-campus academic pursuits. This system, which I call the "different hat" system is common practice among academics who serve on the boards of civil organizations (wearing one hat) and then pursue their scholarly objectivity (wearing another). For example, the excellent research conducted by Molad is not published in academic journals or other academic media but distributed to a list of members. This division delineates what is permissible on campus—leaving the campuses allegedly apolitical supervised spaces. That said, there is one political position that is legitimate on campus: support for the government.

The late Professor Zeev Tzahor, former president of Sapir College, permitted and even encouraged political activism on his campus, which is near the Gaza border. He allowed demonstrations against the war in Gaza even as rockets were flying overhead. Nevertheless, at a conference on the subject of politics on campus in 2009, he explained that politics belongs in the cafeteria and not in the classroom.

I began this chapter with Ido, who told the class about the experience of transgender students in Sheikh Jarrah. Ido, unlike most students who are active off campus, felt safe enough in this class to bring his struggle onto the campus.

The proximity of Sheikh Jarrah to the campus and the involvement of many students and faculty members in demonstrations of support for the evicted families of Sheikh Jarrah, and the ensuing understanding of the importance of meaningful, reciprocal, campus-community partnerships, prompted us to wonder how we could bring the story of the neighborhood onto campus and how the campus might assist the families in their struggle.

We organized two discussion evenings on campus at which the families presented their positions and stories, and legal experts presented possible legal solutions. The hall was filled to bursting. In order to avoid the usual awkwardness of bringing Palestinian guests on to the campus, we brought the residents of Sheikh Jarrah to the campus in private cars with university parking permit stickers. When I entered the Humanities parking lot with four Palestinian women with covered heads in my car, I had a moment's anxiety that I would be questioned as to their identity and reason for entering the campus. But nobody asked, and Um Nabil said with a smile, "We could live here. Look how big this parking lot is. So close to us and we've never been here."

Despite my part in organizing these two events, I too was complicit in the separation of the Sheikh Jarrah struggle from the campus. Even I, who had never believed it possible or necessary to leave politics off campus, did not consider making the Sheikh Jarrah struggle part of one of my courses.

My two children, Gali and Uri Agnon, were among the initiators and leaders of the joint Israeli Palestinian struggle to stop the evictions and return the Palestinians to their homes in Sheikh Jarrah. I joined them at hundreds of protests in Sheikh Jarrah. I watched five policemen break my son's wrist. I cried watching him arrested violently over and over again.[9] My son spent nine weekends locked up in the Russian compound.

In the end, however, the chance to teach our students about Sheikh Jarrah and have them interact with the residents of Sheikh Jarrah came from the United States. There was a big media buzz over the struggle in Sheikh Jarrah. The School of International Law at Duke University approached the Faculty of Law at the Hebrew University proposing collaboration on an academic course on housing in East Jerusalem, especially Sheikh Jarrah. Along with Attorney Sami Ersheid, an expert on housing (or the lack thereof) and house demolition in East Jerusalem, we designed a course about gender and planning. The Israeli students were supposed to learn the legal history as described by the residents, and the American students would study the subject in terms of international law.

Because of Adv. Sami Ersheid's involvement as legal counsel for some of the Palestinian families, and my own involvement, the question of reciprocity between the students and the families became more pronounced. Feminist scholars have written about the "What do I get out of your research?" response of some subjects or interviewees. The relationship between the research subject and the researchers has been the subject of broad discussion among feminist academics. To put it plainly, who benefits from the campus–community interaction?

The spring before the course opened, I sat with Um Nabil on the tiled patio in the yard that was divided between the tent for solidarity activists with the Al Kurd family and the small house built for Nabil and his family that was now home to settlers and their dog. When I mentioned that perhaps next year's law students would come to learn about the legal issues in Sheikh Jarrah, she asked me to go inside and sit in the living room with her. "Flowers lady"—she calls me this because of the flowers I pick from my garden and bring to her on demonstration days—"Will the students come all year? Will they help us get our homes back? Will they get the settlers and their dog out of my son Nabil's house? How will they help?" I could not promise that we would help the families legally and so I tried to think of what benefit we could offer. "Most people only come once," she says, looking out at the full visitors' tent that has been set up in her yard. "Maybe you could prepare a booklet with us. Something we could give them instead of telling our stories over and over." To make this happen and to ensure that the relations between the students and the residents were reciprocal and mutually beneficial, we invited Miki Kratsman and Chen Shapira and their photography students from Bezalel to collaborate with us.

Sami Ersheid arranged a preliminary meeting and moderated the discussion with the men of Sheikh Jarrah to obtain their permission to bring in the students. Amany Khalifa, a social work student and the course teaching assistant, led a preliminary meeting with the women of Sheikh Jarrah. The women said they were concerned that their children had no structured activities for the summer months. Amany agreed to organize a month-long camp for the neighborhood children in a nearby playground. The camp, along with her daily visits and support for the families, won the hearts of the women.

The students documented the stories of the Palestinian families living in fear of eviction and the life stories of the three families who had already been evicted. They asked the residents to say what they perceived justice to be and published their responses in three languages on a website they created and in a booklet entitled *Voices from Sheikh Jarrah*.

In Sheikh Jarrah, the students learned about the discrepancy between law and justice, the distance between the rule of law and reality, and about different perceptions of the legal system. They learned from the residents and joined them in contemplating whether the situation in Sheikh Jarrah could be remedied through the Israeli legal system. Whether, as Audre Lorde put it, the master's tools could dismantle the master's house.[10]

View of Lifta

Chapter 4

LIFTA: SITE FOR RECONCILIATION

Plans for the development of a luxurious neighborhood on the site of the abandoned Palestinian village of Lifta, the remains of which grace the entrance to Jerusalem, were publicized in 2004. Approximately three thousand residents of the village fled during the 1948 war,[1] settling on the outskirts of the village's agricultural lands near the Hebrew University Mount Scopus campus. They were among over seven hundred thousand Palestinians who were displaced or fled in that year. Not permitted to return after the war, they became refugees. What distinguishes Lifta is that, unlike hundreds of other Palestinian villages that were destroyed in the 1950s and 1960s, it was not razed entirely. Fifty-five of Lifta's 450 houses are still standing.

When the Lifta development plan was announced, a nonprofit organization called *Bimkom—Planners for Planning Rights*, petitioned the council for planning and construction to scrap the Lifta project and revisit the issue with public input. One of my students that year was interning with Bimkom. Deciding that it would be interesting to learn how and why the petition to halt the Lifta development had been submitted, we planned a guided walking tour. I could not possibly have prepared myself emotionally for what transpired as we explored the village.[2]

Nili Baruch, a planner from Bimkom, met us at the entrance to the village and mapped out the development plan for construction of over two hundred residential units, a shopping center, and a hotel. With both expertise and humility, she explained Bimkom's opposition to construction in the vicinity of the mosque and cemetery and spoke of the Lifta villagers' right to memory. After parting ways with Nili, we followed refugee Yacoub Odeh as he guided us around the now desolate village in which he was born. He regaled us with tales of his childhood, festive social gatherings beside the spring, the school he attended, which still stands on the hill and is now a school for Jewish children from Romema. He described the thriving agricultural enterprise that revolved around the spring and sustained all the village families. As he spoke, the empty village seemed to ring with the sounds of his childhood. Yacoub also spoke of the day Lifta was abandoned, of his longing, of an entire community's desire to return to their village, and their faith that they will eventually do so.

After taking leave of Yacoub, the 15 Israeli and Palestinian students in the group sat in a circle on the roof of an abandoned house to eat and talk as twilight descended. The conversation was harrowing. Long after the sun had set and the village was clothed in darkness, we remained there on the roof, weeping—some out loud with real tears, some silently. The first to cry was Efrat, an Israeli student who reminded me a lot of myself when I was younger. "Why do you have to blame us?," she asked the Palestinian students, who sat silent and pained. "My grandfather came here from Europe, from the concentration camps. He came here and fought without knowing what was going on. Why do you blame us?"

The Palestinian students were reluctant to speak. "We're sitting here surrounded by pain. How do you expect us to speak here, in this place of pain?" asked one of them. Nevertheless, little by little, we all found our voices. Three Palestinian students expressed their disapproval of Bimkom, an organization that emphasizes the right to memory: "We have no interest in a sign declaring 'Palestinians once lived here'; we want the refugees to return to Lifta." Another student addressed the fracturing of the connections that had been formed between the Jewish and Palestinian students over the year. "If you Jewish students don't help us to bring the refugees back to Lifta—I mean actually show up with a backhoe and help us—then you are no friends of mine." Most of the female Palestinians expressed their desire to remain silent. They had learned not to share their stories beyond the safety of their own homes. "Every one of us has refugee stories but they are not for telling at school or university. These stories of houses that are no more are only to be told at home. Almost every family still has a key to a house that was evacuated in 1948, and we all have unknown relatives who never returned from exile." "Lifta is no different than the hundreds of Palestinian villages destroyed in 1948," said one Palestinian woman through her tears. "We don't want to talk about Lifta as if all those homes in Jaffa and Haifa and Ma'alul and hundreds of other villages never existed." Some of the students said that Yacoub reminded them of their grandfathers. Others, both Israeli and Palestinian, expressed admiration for Bimkom's important work. They reasoned that preserving the memory of this village once inhabited by Palestinians—be it only with a signpost—was preferable to letting it be forgotten forever, as so many other villages were. Most of the Jewish students declared that this was the first time they had heard about the Nakba and that the information was very difficult for them to process. Efrat wept on. After agreeing to meet later that week to continue the conversation, the group walked up the steep path through the darkened village toward the lights of Jerusalem and the nearby central bus station.

Four days after the tour of Lifta, we met at a student's home. This meeting also ended in tears. I began to fear that the discussion had taken an unfortunate turn. I tried to speak about reconciliation and tolerance, but Efrat wept even louder, inconsolable. The Palestinian students, who were all citizens of Israel, said that this was the first time they had ever entered a Jewish home. Some inquired as to the meaning of the names of nearby streets—Rashba, Ramban, and so on, acronyms of the names of important Jewish rabbis.

As before, some Palestinian students wished to remain silent. Other Palestinian students stressed the need for recognition and implementation of the right to return. Yet others asserted that if these rights were never realized, no peace agreement could ever be reached. Some spoke of acknowledgment, others of the need for forgiveness. "I can say that I feel your pain because you have taught me how traumatic the Nakba was for you and it pains me to hear this," said Yoav, an Israeli student. "But I can't apologize because that would be assuming responsibility for your catastrophe and I don't feel responsible. I don't feel willing or able to ask for forgiveness. I can only offer my condolences."

I fell in love with Lifta on that first tour, and I've since accompanied dozens of students and activists on visits to the imperiled village. The white blossoms of the almond trees frosting the valley in winter, the wildflowers blooming in spring, the fig trees heavy with fruit in the summer, and the magnificent empty houses, bear witness to all the Palestinian villages that were abandoned and to the Israeli–Palestinian conflict itself. Lifta, a short and easy walk from the central bus station in Jerusalem, tells a story that has been expunged from Israeli textbooks, campuses, consciousness, maps, and public discourse.

Denial of the Nakba

Over five hundred Palestinian villages were abandoned during the 1948 war and over seven hundred thousand Palestinians[3] were displaced. Not allowed to return to their homes and lands at the end of the war,[4] these refugees constituted the majority of the Palestinian community at the time. Today some 70 percent of Palestinians are refugees and the Nakba, or catastrophe, is to date Palestinian society's most formative event.[5] One major reason that Jewish Israelis deny the Nakba is for fear that the return of Palestinian refugees would threaten the Jewish majority in Israel and the Jewish character of the state.[6] The Israeli education system (in both Hebrew and Arab schools), the academy, the media, and public discourse all perpetuate this denial. In collaboration with Zvika Orr, I conducted a study of human rights organizations in Israel. The results revealed that even organizations that are perceived as left-wing, internalize the denial and intentionally avoid the subject of the Nakba.[7]

Most human rights organizations ignore the Nakba, the 1948 expulsion, and the direct connection Palestinians make between 1948 and 1967. The Oudeh family, for example, left their home in Lifta during the 1948 war and was not allowed to return. Like thousands of Palestinian families, they are refugees. They live in the Shuafat refugee camp where their house is slated for demolition. No Israeli human rights organization is defending their land rights in Lifta or making the connection between their lost home in Lifta and their condemned home in Shuafat.

Generations of Israelis have grown up knowing nothing about the Nakba and the recent past of the state in which they live. Noga Kadman, in her book *Erased from Space and Consciousness*, describes the erasure of Palestinian names from Israeli public space through the renaming of streets, neighborhoods, junctions, and districts. She describes visiting Lifta as a child with school and youth-group field trips: "The visits left me with the vague impression that Lifta was an ancient site, essentially a ruin, as if it had always stood there silent, somewhat mysterious, beautiful and a bit threatening, with its stillness and its narrow alleys between the houses and thickset walls."[8]

I too remember such field trips, with teachers and guides sometimes pointing out a ruin, occasionally using an Arabic name but no other marker of identity. The ruins were never attributed to a Palestinian village that had been destroyed and uprooted; we remained uninformed.[9] When my children were in school, I joined their annual field trip to Nahal Halilim not far from Jerusalem. The guide pointed out the remains of a destroyed Palestinian village, saying that it was a ruin where a sheikh was buried. This sheikh had no name and the ruined village, the remains of which could still be seen, was given no mention. The guide spoke about the wild herbs growing on the banks of the stream as if Palestinians had never lived there.

In addition to the formal and informal education systems' denial of the Palestinian past, Israeli museums also skip over hundreds of years of Arab settlement as if they had never happened.

In his book *Rock, Paper*, Tomer Gardi describes his gradual realization that the museum of history and nature on Kibbutz Dan, where he was born and raised, was built on the rubble of the Arab village that had been there prior to the state.

> What was the village that they built our museum out of? [...] and why, if they had to build a museum from the ruins of a destroyed Arab village—Hunin was its name I eventually found out—[...] is there no mention of this village in our history? Why is there no recollection of the dozens of Arab villages in the Hula valley? Why does the history this museum seeks to construct make out that there are no Arabs here and

never were? [...] Also, perhaps most significantly: how is that erasure, repression, oppression, related to the erasure and oppression of Arabs here and now.[10]

Gardi describes a situation that is not unique to his kibbutz. Several abandoned Palestinian houses were turned into museums that failed to acknowledge the buildings' past or any Palestinian history at all. For example, the museum that occupies a former mosque in the old city of Beer Sheva does not refer to the Arab past of the city. The museum on the Seam in Jerusalem, which prides itself on its human rights agenda, pointedly makes no mention of the fact that it is located in a house that was designed and built by well-known architect Andoni Baramki for his family. The house was appropriated for Jewish public use in 1948. In her book *Golda Slept Here*, Souad Amiri tells the story of Professor Gabi Baramki, president of Birzeit University, paying a visit to this house in which he was born and raised. Not only was his family's history and ownership of the house unacknowledged in the museum's exhibits, but he was asked to buy an entrance ticket.[11] He did not comply.

This is not some momentary oversight on the part of the museum's directorship; it is part of a systematic attempt by political leadership—the Jerusalem municipality and other government ministries—to erase Palestinian history. The following interchange between Menachem Daum, an American director who was producing a movie about Lifta, and Itzik Shweiki, the director of the Jerusalem-based Council for the Conservation of Heritage Sites in Israel, makes this quite clear:

DAUM: At this time of tension in the region, shouldn't we make a symbolic gesture and refrain from developing Lifta?

SHWEIKI: I think you're wrong. I think differently. If I turn this into a monument and say there was an Arab village here, it will only give rise to hatred. Give them Lifta, tomorrow they will want Katamon; give them Katamon, tomorrow they will want Talbiyeh; give them Talbiyeh they'll want Tel Aviv/Jaffa. I'm not willing to do that. We are the State of Israel; we are Jews; we need to be here and leave no trace of Arab heritage.[12]

The denial of the Nakba is profound and insidious. Like Gardi and Kadman who are some twenty years my juniors, I too knew nothing until I came to Jerusalem to study at the Hebrew University. Only then did I hear for the first time about the Palestinian past of the state of Israel. I asked my new friends why their parents lived in Arab houses because I didn't know that before 1948 Katamon and Talbiyeh were Arab neighborhoods.

I was born in Haifa and grew up in Beer Sheva, making it especially disturbing that I had no clue that both cities had once, as recently as in my parents' time, been Arab cities. The Arab aspect of local history was absolutely denied. Arabs, we were told, came after us Jews to the city of the patriarch Abraham. Zionist education at school along with nationalist education at home, and the purposeful erasure of the Palestinian past from the maps and landscapes of Beer Sheva, meant that I would visit my boyfriend's house in the old city of Beer Sheva without making the obvious connection. Beer Sheva's old city seemed ancient to me, from the time of Abraham; its Arab inhabitants were absent from my consciousness. We were taught in school that the city of Beer Sheva was planned by the Germans for the Turks. The Arabs who lived there were absent from collective memory, consciousness, and textbooks. Arabs were also missing from the municipal museum, located in a former mosque, which described the history of Beer Sheva from biblical to contemporary times. This feat of erasure was accomplished by the blatant omission of the last few centuries.[13]

The Nakba was banished from our eyes and ears. I didn't understand that my first boyfriend's home in Beer Sheva was an Arab house until I was in my fifties. The realization came when my friend Jack Persekian showed me artworks from an exhibition that he curated for the Sharjah contemporary art biennial. He paused over a particular work in which, counter to Arab practice, laundry was hanging outside of the house. Jack spoke about the enormous response to this work. At the same time, I remembered the laundry hanging in the internal courtyard of my first boyfriend's house and then I realized with amazement that the house I had visited so often in my youth, with its internal courtyard surrounded by rooms, was an Arab house.

Over the years I learned that most Israelis—even the outstanding students from a wide variety of departments who participated in my course—have never spoken about the Nakba or the meaning of refugee status for the Palestinians. A significant portion of them does not even know that the majority of Palestinians are refugees who abandoned their homes and lands in 1948. The fear of talking about the Nakba and the Palestinian right of return is so deep-seated that every time the word is uttered in class, or even on campus, somebody argues that the conversation isn't heading in a good direction—that discussion of the right to return threatens our very existence. The very mention of the word "Nakba" in class, they believe, threatens the foundations of the state of Israel.

In the course of discussing an article by Oren Yiftachel and Sandy Kedar about the Israel Lands Authority,[14] a geography/law student noted that the data presented in the article were nothing but demagoguery. "What they're saying is unequivocally wrong. The land was empty. There may have been one or two sheikhs who owned land, but when the Jews came here the land was empty. The Palestinians came later." I asked him to prepare a detailed evidence-based argument to present to the class. At the beginning of the next lesson, he declared that in his opinion the topic had been exhausted.

Today even Israelis who oppose the military occupation of the Occupied Territories and perceive themselves as advocates of human rights, or left-wingers, are quite capable of simultaneously calling for an end to the occupation, and civil rights for all Palestinians in Israel, while failing to acknowledge the Palestinian catastrophe of 1948 or the right to return.

Since the 1990s, "new historians" and Zionist historians have been debating questions such as whether the refugees fled in fear, because their leaders instructed them to do so, or because they were expelled by the Israeli army. Other points of contention have arisen concerning whether there was a formal plan to expel the Palestinians or whether the events were largely localized initiatives.[15] Questions of this nature, for example, whether or not a massacre occurred at Tantura, have even reached the courts.[16] Only in the past decade, however, have people begun writing about why Palestinians were not permitted to return to their homes after the war and why and how some villages were completely razed to the ground, eliminated from the physical landscape as well as maps and consciousness. It's hard to fathom how most Israeli children finish high school unaware that they live in a place that was occupied by Arabs until 1948.[17]

There are of course a handful of Israelis who try to expose Nakba denial. The NGO Zochrot, for example, works to "promote awareness and accountability for the ongoing injustices of the Nakba and the reconceptualization of Return as the imperative redress of the Nakba."[18] Would that more Israeli academics would write, as Yehouda Shenhav has, about how "Israel's democracy can never be fully realized if it does not include the history of 1948."

Popular literature, on the other hand, has addressed the Nakba. The book *Khirbet Khizeh* by S. Yizhar, and the eponymous (banned) movie, was the first piece written close to the 1948 war that dealt with the expulsion of the Palestinians from their homes. In his book *Homesick* (*Four Houses and Longing* in its English translation), Eshkol Nevo depicts refugees working as construction workers in their own houses now occupied by Jews. The book, which tells the story of the renovation of a Palestinian house, became a best seller immediately on publication in 2004.[19] The regime of Nakba denial has been forced to contend with cracks in its integrity caused by such popular literature, and also by the NGO Zochrot. But the main evidence of the failure of this denial is that Palestinian citizens of Israel, as well as Palestinians in the diaspora and the Occupied Territories, have not forgotten what happened. Following the Oslo Accords (which ignored the important question of the refugees), Palestinian citizens of Israel, especially the quarter-million who were uprooted from their homes and since live in Arab settlements within Israel and are known as the internal-displaced or the "present absentees," decided to deepen their connection with the abandoned villages. They went back to visit their abandoned villages, clean up cemeteries, and commemorate the Nakba. Among them were the young people of Ikrit, children, and grandchildren of Palestinians who were asked to leave for a few weeks. In 1951, the high court ruled in favor of their petition together with that of Bira'am, to be allowed to return to their village. They are still waiting for this ruling to be implemented while watching their lands taken to settle Jews.[20]

Nakba day, May 15, which is also Israel's Independence Day, has developed into a day of demonstrations and protests demanding the right to return.[21] In response, the Knesset passed the Nakba Act. According to the first draft, the law was meant to "ban any activist or event that related the day of independence of the State of Israel to a day of mourning."[22] After many discussions of the possible ramifications of this law, the sweeping ban was replaced by financial censure. The Nakba law was passed in the Knesset as an amendment to the budget law in March 2011.[23] The law mandates the minister of finance "to reduce the budget of any body that funds activity that marks the day the state was established as a day of mourning or otherwise negating the existence of the state of Israel as a Jewish and democratic state." This legislation reinforces the dominant discourse in Israel, which denies any existence of the Palestinian Nakba. Nevertheless, it seems that had the denial of the Nakba been absolute, there would be no need for such a dangerous law.

Lifta—Jewish Arabs and the Hope for Reconciliation

The village of Lifta stands desolate and magnificent at the entrance to Jerusalem. Why was it not obliterated like hundreds of other Palestinian villages? I believe that, like the Jewish custom of leaving an unpainted patch on the ceiling to recall the destruction of the temple, Lifta is left to remind us of a destroyed world and the hope that Jews and Arabs might learn to coexist. In fact, Lifta was spared because Jews who came from Arab countries were settled in the abandoned village. Having lost their homes in Iraq and lived for decades in homes lost by Arabs from Lifta, these Jewish Arabs hold one of the keys to the resolution of the Israeli–Palestinian conflict. Lifta would be a worthy location for future truth and reconciliation talks—between Israelis and Palestinians, Jews and Arabs, Ashkenazi Jews and Jewish-Arabs.

In 1949, the state settled immigrants from Yemen in Lifta. In 1951, it was the turn of thousands of Jews from Iraq and also hundreds of immigrants from Iraqi Kurdistan. At the time there was no running water or electricity in

Lifta and conditions were crowded. In the 1960s, all the Yemenite immigrants decided to leave Lifta and move to alternative housing provided by the state. The army ripped a hole in the roof of each vacated house to prevent it from being reinhabited. In 2006, when the Lifta development plan was approved, there were 13 Jewish families from Iraqi Kurdistan still living on the outskirts of the village alongside the Jerusalem-Tel Aviv highway. These families were served eviction notices because the houses had never been registered in their names, they were technically squatters.

Yoni Yochanan, whose family was settled in Lifta in 1951, was born and raised there. He took it upon himself to organize most of the Jewish families in Lifta to resist being evicted as uncompensated squatters. He dedicated years of his life to learning about the settlement of Lifta. He found letters of support for the immigrants from Rachel Ben Zvi, wife of the president at the time, and lists of worshippers in Lifta's synagogues to prove that the families had lived, rightfully, in Lifta for decades.

More than anything, it pained Yoni to see his terminally ill father, who had lost his house, lands, and property once before in Kurdistan, evicted yet again. Some months before he died, Yochanan Matlub told his son Yoni the story of his journey from a home in Iraq to a home in Lifta. "I bought the house from a Yemenite. I paid more for this closet than for the house." Speaking in Arabic, Matlub told Yaacov Oudeh, Palestinian refugee and activist in the coalition to save Lifta, about the warm relations that were established after 1967 between the Palestinian owners and the Matlub family. He spoke about long-standing friendship that developed following the first visit, how they welcomed each other at family gatherings and how he identified with them because he too had left a home in Iraq in a village very similar to Lifta. He spoke longingly of that village and the good relations he had enjoyed with his Muslim neighbors.

Minister of Finance Moshe Kahalon was personally involved in the historical agreement reached with the Jewish residents of Lifta, who did vacate their homes in summer 2017. At a moving ceremony in March 2017, the residents and state signed an agreement. Speaking at the event Kahalon said that the story of Lifta was the story of his own family and of many Jewish families that had come to Israel from Arab countries and whose contribution to the state had never been recognized. He promised to help families facing eviction after being settled in abandoned Palestinian houses. Yoni Yochanan, who championed the cause of the families from Kurdistan who were settled in Lifta, conducted longitudinal archive research and found that the reason many of the immigrants from Arab countries had not registered their ownership of the homes was illustrative of their poor treatment by the state. The notification regarding official registration of the homes was published exclusively in the newspaper *Davar*—an organ of the Mapai Labor Party—in 1953.

Jews from Arab countries were simply not aware of it, while immigrants from Europe who lived in abandoned Palestinian homes in Talbiyeh, Katamon, and other affluent neighborhoods, were regular readers of *Davar*. The Jewish Arab residents of Lifta were eventually evicted in 2017 but as "pioneers" rather than squatters, with the concomitant recognition and compensation. Even so, these evacuees fear that the village will become a ghost town, with luxury vacation homes owned by rich Jews from Western countries obliterating this beautiful oasis so beloved by the residents of Jerusalem.

In 2011, following the issue of the public tender for the development of Lifta, a group of Israeli and Palestinian activists formed the coalition to save Lifta. The coalition includes architects and planners concerned with preserving the structural heritage of Lifta, refugees from Lifta who sought to protect their propriety over the village and their right to return there at some point in the future, environmentalists opposed to the destruction of the natural landscape, and human rights activists, both Israeli and Palestinian. We were joined by representatives of the Jewish families from Kurdistan and Iraq who were living in Lifta.

The coalition petitioned the high court, seeking to stop the tender until an archeological survey of Lifta had been completed. The petition also noted the "historical stripping of rights from the original residents of the village" who had "historical rights of propriety that had never been severed."[24] In February 2012, the court accepted the petition and canceled the tender.

The court ordered the state to survey Lifta before selling the land but did not address the land ownership question. According to Israeli law, all the lands of Lifta were declared abandoned property, as were the vast majority of lands owned by the hundreds of thousands of Palestinians who were expelled or fled during the 1948 war. While the court enables Jews to reclaim property that was theirs before 1948, as is the case in nearby Sheikh Jarrah, Israeli law does not permit Palestinians to reclaim the property that they lost in 1948. This stalled the development plan, if only temporarily. The court victory also did not ameliorate the desire of municipal and national leaders to make Lifta disappear—to erase Palestinian history.

Israeli law does not permit the refugees from Lifta to reclaim their lands even if they reside in nearby Jerusalem. The small administrative affairs courtroom in the city was packed to the limit with refugees from Lifta on the day that attorney Sami Ersheid asked the court, in Hebrew, on behalf of the petitioners, myself included, to stop the development plan. The court translator was on her feet throughout the discussion, translating into Arabic for some fifteen elders from Lifta who were sitting squashed into the courtroom benches, wearing traditional cloaks. Though they filled the courtroom, these people were conspicuously absent from the verdict.

In response to the court's ruling, the state committed itself to conducting an archeological and environmental survey within three months. Performed by the Antiquities Authority, this survey took five years and was the most expensive and extensive ever conducted in Israel. The results reflect the historical, archeological, architectural, and environmental wealth that is unique to the village. Architect Avi Mashiach, the lead researcher, explained at a conference held at Bezalel[25] that the survey of Lifta had found historical evidence predating the First Temple period and he hoped "that the results of the survey would lead to preservation of the village for posterity." He warned that the development project endangered one of the most important natural springs in the Jerusalem area. Contradicting claims that the houses in the village were derelict and in danger of collapse, Mashiach explained that this was true of only 5 percent of the buildings and that all of them could be preserved. "It needs to be a slow process, step-by-step one-house-at-a-time, using the original technology." But Mashiach made it clear that the survey was conducted on a warrant from the court to facilitate issuing a reworked tender rather than to derail the development plan. Nevertheless, the fact remains that the development of Lifta is politically rather than professionally motivated.

The plan to destroy Lifta to make way for 200 residential units for the top 0.01 percent was clearly not devised to ease any residential shortage in Jerusalem, but rather to erase the last memory of the Palestinians who fled in 1948. Thus, the unlikely alliance between the ultraorthodox members of the municipal planning committee and activists on behalf of public and accessible housing in Jerusalem, who joined forces to oppose the development plan because it is not likely to reduce the serious housing shortage in the city.

The struggle to save Lifta coincided with the popular social justice movement that emerged in Israel. The movement organized itself around the housing shortage and its motto "home is a tent" to protest the prevalence of homelessness in Israel.

The main tent camp on Rothschild Boulevard in Tel Aviv was established by Daphne Lief, a student protesting the exorbitant cost of housing in Tel Aviv. She was soon joined by thousands and camps sprang up all over the country. In Jerusalem, there were two: the students camped in Horse Park and the homeless camped in Independence Park. Dozens of families who had been thrown out of their homes for defaulting on their rent lived in Independence Park for months. Most of them were women and children, third-generation poor, with roots in Arab countries and the former Soviet Union. In all the tent camps, including in Horse Park, the discussion focused on affordable housing. The dominant voices in this protest were those of young people and students who couldn't afford rental costs. Academics like Yossi Yona and Avihu Spivak offered their services to translate the protest into a plan.[26] At its height, hundreds of thousands of people were involved in the movement. In response, the prime minister appointed the chair of the Council for Higher Education, Prof. Manuel Trajtenberg, to head a public commission charged with handling the movement's demands. The middle-class young people were heard and received many promises, only a small portion of which have been kept: mainly free preschool education until age 3. At the beginning of winter, when the main tent camp in Tel Aviv packed up, the students left the tent camp in Horse Park in Jerusalem. Twenty homeless families remained in Independence Park. They demanded the addition of units to public housing so that those eligible would not have to wait years for a place. Because no one was listening and because the beginning of the rainy season made it very difficult to maintain the tent camp, the families moved into empty apartments in Jerusalem under the slogan "no empty apartments when children are homeless." At a time when the student protest and homeless protest had almost parted ways, the latter dovetailed with the struggle to protect Lifta—the connective node being the Mizrahi Jews demand for equal rights in a state that has discriminated against them since the 1950s and continues to do so. It was Yoni Yochanan who made connections between these activists and the immigrants who had been settled in Lifta based on their common experience of being threatened with eviction.

In the film *Salah, This Is Israel*, Dudu Deri exposes the population distribution that forced immigrants from Arab countries into the periphery of Israel—on lands abandoned by Palestinians in 1948. Almost 80 percent of the Jewish population was concentrated in cities and the Jewish Arabs were settled in abandoned villages and development towns. While veteran Israelis purchased the apartments they lived in, immigrants from Arab countries were given "public housing," which they were not permitted to purchase. Deri also shows how the Polish Jews, who arrived in 1956 and 1957, were given ownership of homes built for them in Ramat Aviv.[27]

One of the first structures taken over by a tent community called "Ein Brera" (No Choice) was a 64-apartment building in Kiryat Yovel. Owned by the Hebrew University, it had stood empty for years. A dozen families with small children and a handful of student activists moved into the empty apartments. The university declared that the apartments were designated for dormitories and the police brutally evicted the families. The most upsetting part for me, after weeks in the Ein Brera tent camp in Independence Park and many days in the apartments watching the police evict families over and over again in the summer, fall, and winter of 2011, was that they were being evicted from a building owned by the university. Though the apartments have since been renovated and are now occupied by medical students studying on the Ein Karem campus, the university missed a valuable opportunity to build cooperative relations with the community. The single mothers who had moved in from the tent camp had suggested, to no avail, that the university dedicate 20 of the 128 apartments in the two buildings to single mothers who had been waiting years for public housing.

Etti Hen, one of the leaders of the single mothers' struggle for public housing, told me at the first meeting we organized at the university, "I never dreamed I would ever get to visit the university." Since 2014, Etti Hen has been the coordinator at the Katamonim center of the Human Rights clinic operated by the Hebrew University Faculty of Law. Along with law students and lawyers, the clinic assists hundreds and women and men realize their rights to public housing.

From South Africa to Lifta

After touring Lifta with my students in 2004, I suggested that we look at other conflict scenarios, for example, the South African Truth and Reconciliation Commission, as a model for thinking about Lifta and our shared past and futures in this place. I tried to communicate to the students that the future could look different in order to imbue them with some hope.

To my mind, the District 6 museum in Cape Town is one of the models most relevant to Lifta. District 6 was a neighborhood in the heart of Cape Town where blacks, whites, Jews, and Indians lived peaceably until the apartheid government declared it a whites-only area in the 1960s. Over sixty thousand people were displaced and all the buildings, except for the large Methodist Church, were razed. In their place, a technical college for whites only was built and a large swathe of land remains empty to this day. With the fall of the apartheid regime, the church was turned into a museum. The lifestyles that flourished in the area before the demolition of the neighborhood are presented. The museum serves as an educational center and memorial to the neighborhood, which was erased by the Forced Removals Act. It is visited by thousands of schoolchildren, tourists, and others, and also serves as a support center for residents who wish to return to District 6. About one hundred of the removed families have received new homes in the neighborhood. The rebuilding of District 6 is happening in cooperation with the people who were removed from it.

The District 6 museum both preserves the memory of the area and plays a role in its reconstruction. In like fashion, Lifta could serve as a memorial to Palestinian life before and after the Nakba[28] and also to the history of immigrants from Yemen and Iraqi Kurdistan who were settled there. Preservation of the village as a historical and educational resource might

Abandoned homes in Lifta

make it possible for some of the refugees to return in the future—as was the case in South Africa.

The purpose of the comparison with apartheid is to engender hope for a shared future between Israelis and Palestinians. The analogy derives from my long-standing personal relationship with South Africa; I traveled there in 1984 to conduct research for my doctoral dissertation.[29]

Comparison of Israel to apartheid South Africa raises questions similar to those that confronted the directors of the District 6 museum. How can the area be preserved and the return of the residents be facilitated? Who will return? Who will decide who returns? There are 55 houses left in Lifta and 30,000 Palestinians who see themselves as refugees from Lifta.

Is Israel an Apartheid State?

In the late 1970s, as a student of African Studies at the Hebrew University of Jerusalem, I took a course called "Introduction to South African History." The lecturer drew two concentric circles on the board and told us "South Africa is like these two concentric circles. About 5 million whites live in the inner circle in a democracy. They elect their parliament democratically in free elections and they have a justice system and free press. The outer circle is home to some 30 million black people who have no rights whatsoever."

I wondered how this could be, asking exactly where the dividing line ran. How could the circumstances of those in the inner circle differ so extremely from those in the outer circle? What would happen if a white woman married a black man under these circumstances? "It seldom happens" was the response I received. "Mixed marriages are against the law. Whites and blacks cannot marry." "What about if a white journalist wanted to report on events in the outer circle? Is that possible?" "There is censorship in South Africa, whatever is perceived as a threat to state security is censored. There is legislation in place that enables the minister of home affairs to close down papers that don't abide by the rules, but it rarely happens. White newspapers in South Africa are not likely to violate censorship laws." "What about a political party advocating for black rights," I pushed, "Could people vote for it like any other party in the South African democracy?" "Some parties are banned. There is legislation that forbids, for example, any communist gathering."

Even then, all those years ago, I found this "democracy for whites only" concept hard to grasp. I have never managed to envision or understand this imaginary line that divides those with rights from those without. The double moral standards of white South Africa, shored up by denial, are reminiscent of the so-called liberal stance in Israel, which distinguishes between the Jewish democratic state and its Occupied Territories.

As was the case in apartheid South Africa, Israeli liberals still believe that they live in a democracy because of the precise and consistent use of a system of laws that normalizes the abnormal discriminatory reality and makes it possible to enforce different sets of laws for different groups. Both regimes anchored discriminatory policy in complex legal labyrinths operationalized by a well-oiled army of lawyers, courts, and massive bureaucracies.

Like apartheid South Africa, Israel employs hundreds of lawyers and legal advisors in the service of explaining the legality of injustice. In addition to the use of law as a means of facilitating the division between those who enjoy democracy and those who ("in the meantime") have no basic rights, both the apartheid government and the Israeli regime have rewritten history and cultivated immense military strength in order to safeguard their discriminatory policies.

Israel may bear many resemblances to South Africa, but it is also quite different. Before I return to Lifta, I proffer a brief outline of the significant differences between Israel and apartheid South Africa.

In the first place, in South Africa, a small minority controlled the national resources and withheld rights from the majority. Even though Israel has controlled millions of Palestinians in the Occupied Territories for 50 years, it is still perceived as a democratic country. This is because it does grant civil rights to a small group of Palestinians who live inside the Green Line. This "geographic magic garden," as Stanley Cohen called it, enables Israelis, including liberals and legal professionals, to adhere to the view that Israel is a democratic and Jewish state. The Green Line—which Israel erased from the maps as early as 1970 and does not recognize as an international border—is the imaginary line that enables Israelis to preserve the "Jewish majority" while continuing to claim that theirs is a democratic country.

However, the numbers of Jews and Arabs in Israel and the Occupied Territories combined are almost equivalent.[30] The law still gives Jews more rights than Arabs. In fact, the Arab population is divided into several subgroups that have different levels of rights: Palestinians in the West Bank, Palestinians in Gaza, and Palestinians in Jerusalem. Others, Palestinians who are Israeli citizens, enjoy almost full rights. The apartheid leaders, too, claimed that the whites were a majority in South Africa. Ran Greenstein explains that the

> basic idea behind the Bantustan policy was to define the rights of the indigenous population on a tribal basis, thus ensuring that the whites remain a majority population group (with full rights). This objective required two moves. First, the African majority was splintered into numerous minority groups, sorted by ethnic community, language, culture and political aspirations of its own, which could all be realized in its

"own" territory. Thus, the black majority ceased to exist and everyone became associated with a minority group. Second, South Africa denied the demands of black Africans for political rights in South Africa, claiming that they had other national affiliations. As members, ostensibly of other "nations: and citizens of other 'states' they were not considered part of the South African nation and there also had no rights or benefits in South Africa."[31]

The enormous numeric advantage of blacks over whites in South Africa made it difficult to sustain the inequality for the long term. In Israel, by contrast, there is no obvious demographic divide. This is not a minority oppressing a majority. There are about 1,900,000 Palestinian citizens of Israel, and 6.6 million Jews. In the West Bank, Jerusalem, and Gaza, there are about 4.8 million Palestinians under Israeli rule. In other words, the numbers of Jews and Arabs are comparable.

The second difference between Israel and South Africa is affirmed by the Jewish–Arab population balance in Israel and Palestine. Advocates of the segregation in South Africa saw the black people as "a group of racially inferior but useful people whose workforce was essential for the survival of the society and economy ruled by the whites."[32] Blacks worked as servants in white homes and shared intimate moments with them. They were present in white cities and homes—as an oppressed workforce, but present. In Israel on the other hand, the segregation policy is such that Israelis rarely encounter Palestinians. The number of Palestinians who work in Israel is negligible. Most Palestinians from the Occupied Territories are not allowed into Israel. Thus, Israelis cannot see the daily humiliations experienced by Palestinians in the Occupied Territories.

In his remarkable book *A Dry White Season*, South African author Andre Brink depicts the upheaval experienced by a white family that witnesses the suffering and humiliation of its black gardener's family.[33] In Israel, Palestinian gardeners are less and less common. The network of walls, fences, checkpoints, and prohibitions keeps Palestinians from finding employment within Israel. As Myra Hammermesh demonstrated in her film *Maids and Madams*,[34] despite all the racism, white women in South Africa commonly left their most precious belonging, their children, in the care of black nannies. This kind of relationship is almost nonexistent in today's Israel. Interactions between Jewish and Palestinian Israeli citizens are few and far between. University campuses are the loci of the first encounter with the other for most Jews and Palestinians, coming as they do from completely segregated school systems. And even on campus, opportunities for discussion and familiarization are few. My Palestinian and Jewish students report at the end of each year that the human rights program was their first and only opportunity on campus to talk to students of the other group.

The third significant difference between the two countries is the role religion plays in each. The Afrikaner settlement myth was based on the biblical belief that they were the chosen people in a promised land. The apartheid regime invoked the biblical paradigm as a justification of white settlement in South Africa. The Calvinist Afrikaners who had come to the "dark" continent fleeing religious persecution in Europe saw the Africans as needing a separate developmental space. But despite the apartheid regime having grounded itself in this unique perception of Christianity, Christianity also played an important role in the healing and reconciliation process that took place in South Africa in the 1990s. In contradistinction, the flames of the Israeli–Arab conflict are fueled by Jewish–Muslim tensions, with no hint of a reconciliatory inclination on either side. The religious conflict is no metaphor, but a genuine face-off at the most sacred heart of all three monotheistic religions: Jerusalem. The religious struggle for the Temple Mount, between Jews and Muslims, who each deny the other's claim to the site, is a trope for the entire Arab–Israeli conflict and one of the main factors lending this conflict momentum. The Calvinist Afrikaners adopted the biblical narrative about the chosen people returning to their homeland. In Israel, the biblical story that is definitive of its nationhood, constitutes, according to the Zionists, even stronger justification of ownership over the land.

The fourth difference between Israel and apartheid South Africa is the role played by the international community. A cultural boycott was imposed on apartheid South Africa and it was expelled from all international cultural and sporting forums, economic sanctions were put in place and investors encouraged to avoid any dealings with South Africa, even indirect ones. Israel, on the other hand, receives billions of dollars of support from the United States, participates in European sporting events as well as the Olympic Games, and the condemnations frequently heard in the UN have not been translated into economic sanctions. Palestinian and international efforts to call for a boycott of Israel are gathering momentum but until now the boycott, divestment, and sanctions (BDS) movement has not managed to isolate Israel as it did South Africa.

The BDS movement has been successful mainly in the academic arena. Recently the number of high-profile academics attending conferences in Israel has dropped. Some of them, Judith Butler, for example, explain why they choose to boycott Israeli institutions and visit only Palestinian universities. Some decline participation in Israeli events on the pretext of being otherwise engaged. Some simply ignore the invitations. The issue of whether to participate in Israeli conferences comes up repeatedly, as it does for musicians and artists invited to appear. Whatever the answer may be, the question resonates among us, Israeli academics.

In South Africa, the academic boycott was extremely significant. South African lecturers were not invited to international conferences and most of the Western academic world shunned South African universities. Twenty years of increasingly strong boycott caused dozens of South African academics into exile, many of whom returned years later to teach in the universities of the new South Africa.

The boycott of South Africa was born in the universities of Europe and the United States, and the call to boycott Israel is coming from the same campuses. When I was a student in the 1980s, I participated in hundreds of demonstrations supporting the boycott of South Africa. One of the significant achievements of the movement was when the senate of University of California, Berkeley, along with all public universities in California, withdrew $9.2 billion from banks that had investments in South Africa. The boycott movement began with students and citizens filling supermarket trolleys with South African products and leaving them at the checkout counters. Soon, the demonstrations turned violent, for example, the one protesting the South African cricket team's participation in matches in Australia. The civil protest was joined by the UN and heads of state. Israel, in contrast, is still receiving full support and backup from the United States and European countries, despite growing anti-occupation activism on campuses and in cities.

And the fifth and final difference between Israel and South Africa is that the latter had a shared vision of a united country, while the former is envisioned, in the eyes of most Israelis and Palestinians as well as the international community, as two separate states. The anti-apartheid movement was committed to a joint struggle against apartheid and a shared life in the new South Africa for both blacks and whites. In Israel and Palestine, there are very few shared areas of activism, with even the Palestinian BDS movement, which advocates a single binational state, firmly opposed to joint Israeli Palestinian endeavors.

Despite these differences, and the current violence and difficulties in South Africa, the enormous change that took place in South Africa with the fall of apartheid is proof, in my opinion, that oppressive regimes can fall even if they rely on enormous military strength, and that emphatic calls for equality can have results.

How can we preserve Lifta as a memorial and at the same time work toward the future return of its refugees? Many sites in Israel reconstruct history, such as Ein Yael in southeast Jerusalem, which operates as a visitor education center for learning about ancient traditional labor methods. Reconstruction of traditional agriculture, utilization of the spring waters, and the historical terraces that the second president of Israel Yitzhak Ben Zvi marveled at and saw as a renewal of biblical agriculture could be the key. Lifta could be all this and more, one of the important green spaces in the city, a center for education about the Nakba and shared Palestinian and Israeli history, a testament to the story of the Jews from Arab countries who were settled there, and a venue for truth and reconciliation events. And finally, it could also be the place to which the refugees of the village return.[35]

Today, when the Nakba law has been passed to silence any mention of the Nakba, it is difficult to believe that Lifta will remain an open, living museum for the study of Nakba and the ripping of Palestinians from their lands. It is even harder to believe that any of the Palestinian refugees will be allowed to return. But in 1989, when they began building the District 6 museum, it must have taken an awful lot of hope to believe that the museum would be inaugurated in 1994, in the New South Africa, and that it would help the displaced to return home. We can dream about truth and reconciliation commissions being convened in Lifta but, in the meantime, the word "reconciliation," along with the word "peace," has been redacted from the shared Israeli–Palestinian lexicon. So has the word "hope." I propose learning a lesson from the joint black–white struggle against apartheid in South Africa so that we can begin remembering what it feels like to hope and be inspired to push the boundaries of the boycott on cooperating with Israelis. The struggle to save Lifta is a test case that requires a collaborative effort from Israelis and Palestinians, as well as the international community, in order to remember the past, change the present, and build a different future.

The archeology building

Chapter 5

STUDENTS WORKING FOR CHANGE: CAMPUS-COMMUNITY PARTNERSHIPS

In summer 2001, at the height of the second Intifada, over six hundred students applied to the Minerva Human Rights Fellowship program. We only had space for 15. At a loss as to how to select 15 students, I consulted with my friend (and relative) Jonah Rosenfeld, Israel Prize laureate for social work and a pioneer of the field in Israel. Jonah, who developed the "learning from success" model, suggested that we analyze the success of the program and try to identify elements that could be replicated in developing similar programs on campus as well as on other campuses. He proposed interviewing the 70 most promising candidates to learn about their motivation. These interviews revealed that there were two main motivating factors for the widespread interest. The first was that the program offered a unique opportunity to engage in human rights work in an academic context. The second was that the two-year-old program had already garnered a reputation for being accessible to Arab students. At the time, the program's recruiting posters were the only ones that appeared in Arabic on the campus bulletin boards. Candidates also identified three areas of interest: children's rights, women's rights (primarily the struggle against sexual violence) and rights pertaining to the Israeli–Palestinian conflict.

In 2001, Jonah and I enlisted about 20 lecturers, students and social activists to participate in a think tank that would contemplate the ideal campus-community relationship. One of the directions proposed was to develop more courses that integrate theory and practice at Hebrew University and also on campuses throughout the country. We visited universities in the United States and in Europe to delve deeper into the theory and practice behind campus-community programs. In 2004–2005, we conducted a study on nine campuses in Israel. Student activists from various social engagement programs were asked which areas they were active in, what they gained from their involvement, and what could be done to enhance the experience.[1] We found students who were eager to make a difference, yet felt that their social activism—whether with Perah, the Unit for Social Involvement, or others—was not acknowledged, studied, spoken of, or appreciated on campus. We interviewed students in various university settings who volunteered in exchange for scholarships. We intentionally did not interview students who were active in student political groups because we wanted to see where the higher education system in Israel is spending the millions of shekels it allocates to social involvement of students.

On all nine campuses, students spoke of a total disjuncture between their social involvement and their studies. A student named Shahar from Sapir College told us: "I'm studying sociology and psychology and I volunteer at a shelter for at-risk girls in Sderot. I don't see any connection between the two."[2] We presented the results of the study at a conference of the Council for Higher Education and consequently ran workshops, study groups, and seminars on the academy's commitment to social change and ways to link academic knowledge with student social engagement. In 2006, we established the Campus-Community Partnership ("the Partnership") in the Hebrew University's Faculty of Law. The Partnership has been instrumental in the development of dozens of community-engaged courses, at 15 universities and colleges, based on the Minerva model of integrating theoretical study with human rights and social justice activism.[3]

The majority of institutions of higher education in Israel have now developed community-engaged programs that integrate theory and practice. This aligns with the international trend toward reaffirming the social commitment of institutions of higher learning. More and more institutions are committed to fostering student volunteerism through community-engaged courses and programs that link academic learning with activism in disadvantaged communities, helping students become active citizens who participate in the democratic process.[4]

Scholars and institutions often base their support for academic social involvement on the philosophy of John Dewey, which emphasizes the strong reciprocal relations between democracy and education and advocates for learning through doing.[5] The university was at one time considered the "prophet of democracy"[6] and the current trend is viewed by many as a return to the traditional role of institutions of higher education as advocates of democratic values, civic engagement, and fundamental social agendas.[7]

Some scholars claim that the troubling state of democracy today can be attributed to a lack of accessible platforms for political involvement.[8] Campus-community partnerships and the like can provide such everyday platforms. The partnerships' emphasis on democratic values turns student volunteers into social justice activists and transforms institutions of higher learning into agents of social change.[9]

Thus far, most research on campus-community partnerships has focused on the impact on students, finding it long-term and robust.[10] Studies conducted in the United States show that students who were active during their time in university were more successful after graduation. Social activism during their studies had a positive effect on their academic achievements, their leadership skills, and self-confidence, and increased the likelihood of their choosing a community-oriented career. The studies show the importance of group discussions in the social involvement experience facilitated by community-engaged courses, and the essential role played by faculty in the whole process.[11] Such courses improve comprehension of theoretical materials, foster better relations among students and also between students and lecturers, and engender a sense of civic obligation in students.[12] Moreover, longitudinal studies have indicated that students involved in these programs have increased motivation to pursue advanced studies and a higher propensity to espouse pluralistic views.[13]

Studies also show a positive correlation between social involvement during studies and a lifelong commitment to social justice activism.[14] Social involvement brings students into contact with disadvantaged groups that they would otherwise never encounter[15]—an enriching, albeit sometimes threatening and troubling, experience. It challenges students' preconceptions about themselves, others and the societies in which they live. The research suggests that reflective discussion in class enhances the students' ability to process such experiences.[16]

Perah is the biggest scholarship program in Israel, funded by the state for over forty years. The program has over twenty thousand Israeli students mentoring individual children in exchange for half of their tuition ($1,500). Together with Limor Goldner, Hala Mashood, and Maya Vardi, I conducted a study on the long-term impact of student participation in scholarship programs of social involvement. The sample consisted of over eight hundred graduates of Ben Gurion University, the Hebrew University, and Sapir College. We compared the experiences of undergraduates who were involved in the Perah mentoring program and had individual supervision, with those who volunteered through the social involvement units and had group supervision.[17] Findings showed that the group setting was the single most influential factor in shaping the students' understanding of their social involvement, and in predicting their future activism. Females reported that the group dimension enhanced their experience as well as the quality of the work they did. This finding is commensurate with findings from other studies on the structures of female student activism. These studies show that students who work in groups (rather than individually) are more deeply influenced by their activism.

The enormous importance of reflection, and of frameworks that facilitate reflection, is borne out by research.[18] Belonging to a group of peer volunteers who are having similar experiences allows for contemplation, sharing, and introspection.[19]

Students who had worked in group settings felt they had undergone a process of personal empowerment. They described addressing challenges and handling unanticipated difficulties as learning experiences that gave them a sense of accomplishment. Interviewees described the consolidation of a professional identity, development of self-confidence and ethical, social, and political awareness. Moreover, group discussions about social issues, in which they were able to express themselves as individuals, contributed to their sense of personal growth and development.

In the Perah Prevention of Sexual Violence program, students facilitate workshops on the subject in schools in both West and East Jerusalem. Israeli students give the workshops in Hebrew in West Jerusalem and Palestinian students do the same in Arabic in East Jerusalem. This is one of the few Perah group programs.[20]

Every summer, incoming volunteers participate in an accelerated training course provided by the collaborating aid agencies. This is the only prerequisite for student participation in the mentoring program in schools. Hebrew and Arabic courses are run separately at each agency. Most of the graduates who participate in the Perah Prevention of Sexual Violence program, in collaboration with the rape crisis shelters, are socially active in other contexts as well. They recall the volunteer experience, particularly in the group setting, as a source of strength and significant personal change.

All the interviewees who volunteered at rape crisis shelters spoke at length about the intimate and open peer group that emerged during the center's training course, which provided them with support throughout the year. The training course combines study of content that students will deliver in schools and personal processing of complex questions about sexuality, gender, and the prevention of violence.

The ongoing reflection group meetings provided by the rape crisis centers and some of the social involvement units were highly regarded as a model. This is a close approximation of the community-engaged courses that research has found to be the most beneficial type of involvement for both students and the community.[21]

The immense investment required of the crisis centers must also be acknowledged. Even though some programs lacked the resources to offer such comprehensive and enabling group supervision, the students spoke of the centers as a second home. Cooperation between Perah's bureaucratic support and the comprehensive group supervision provided by the centers is a model worthy of emulation. In a series of study days, we shared the results of our research with all the partners in the study, including the leaders of Perah. The cooperation between Perah and the rape crisis centers became a model in which students had both training and ongoing support and reflection throughout the year. In 2019, Perah initiated a pilot with the aim of including training and group supervision for some 20 percent of Perah students.

Group reflection is most important to students for several reasons. It allows them to reflect with other student activists about their challenges and fears, and to celebrate success with other young people who are active—whether they are active together or separately—but who all share visions of change and hope. It also allows them to meet people in the communities around the campus—people who are often less fortunate than them. As Etti Chen, the leader of the "single mothers struggle for public housing," stated when she first visited the beautiful Givat Ram Hebrew University campus, "I did not know that I could even dream of visiting a university."

Only about 40 percent of Israeli youth (Jews and Arabs) earn high school diplomas that qualify them to apply to institutions of higher education.[22] In many cases, students who are part of the elite are unaware of the inequality inherent in the education system, their privileged position, and the correlation between parents' socioeconomic status and their children's chances of obtaining a higher education.[23]

Eden was an excellent law student in the Minerva Human Rights program who volunteered at the Jerusalem Open House for Pride and Tolerance. He led a very successful gay pride parade that year. He was a charming young man, who nevertheless insisted in class discussions that "Mizrahi parents don't care about the education of their children," and that the second or third generation of Jewish migrants from Arab countries (Mizrahim) should "stop complaining and start taking responsibility for their situation, and act to improve their lives and get out of poverty themselves, without help from the state or others."

Years after graduating, Eden wrote me a letter to say that he finally understood my lessons about structural inequality in education. "These days, I am a graduate student in London," he wrote, "I am mentoring a refugee child from Sudan. I encouraged him and told him that if he wants, he could be a lawyer like me. My supervisor asked me what I think the chances of this refugee child becoming a lawyer are, and it was then, only then, that I thought about your teaching, and about our discussions on inequality in education, and I realized how young and naïve I was to say the things I said then."

When students meet with people living in poverty, without understanding the sociopolitical context, their biased perceptions can be reinforced. Many times, students refer to people living in poverty as those "who don't try hard enough," who spend money on what students find to be unnecessary like big TV screens or hairstyling, and that "if only they wanted to" they could get out of their poverty and provide their children with a good education.

Overall, students found the encounter with the community very significant, if often upsetting element. The main difference between the Perah program and the group programs of the units for social involvement is that in the latter the group discussions allow students to understand the social and political context of their activism, thus making it possible for them to learn that there are patterns of social inequality and that they are serving the underserved communities instead of social or educational services which failed to do so.[24]

The vast majority of students reported feeling that they contributed, saying, "I made a difference," I gave, I helped, I pushed, I was an example. There were almost no references to reciprocity and mutual enrichment. These were unidirectional relations in which they, as students with tools and skills at their disposal, were giving to those they perceived as needy. The students felt the community labeled them as different and powerful, labels they seemed to accept, or felt unable to correct. The Jewish-Israeli students spoke about their contribution to the particular child they had mentored; the Palestinian students emphasized their contribution to society as a whole. Palestinian students spoke about their contribution to society, and about their desire to bring about change.

Palestinian Graduates Felt They Contributed and Benefitted More

Palestinian graduates felt that their activism as students had more impact on the community; they also felt more enriched by the undertaking than the Israeli students did. Asked to summarize their experience in social activism, the most frequent words of Palestinian students were: rewarding, good, beautiful, and rich. When asked to summarize their overall academic experience, they characterized it as tiring, difficult, and frustrating. Activism gave the Palestinian students' entire academic experience a richness and significance that were otherwise missing.

The students saw their activism as a means of developing and implementing their abilities and talents. Even more importantly, the interaction with fellow Palestinians is an opportunity to strengthen their personal and collective identities, neither of which is acknowledged or evident on campus.

Palestinian students who volunteered in Jerusalem reported developing a sense of belonging in the city. The majority of them had moved to Jerusalem to pursue their studies, and volunteering in the community helped them feel connected. They spoke of getting to know the city and how volunteering allowed them to develop a deeper connection to it.

Jadah, a Perah student from Hebrew University said:

> I come from the north and I knew nothing about Jerusalem. I didn't know about the difficult conditions the Palestinians live under. But when I came and saw, through Perah, what was going on, I developed a sense of solidarity with these families. I always wonder what I can do to improve their situations, even in a simple or small way.

Students who volunteered in the Negev region also reported developing a growing awareness of the sociopolitical issues that impact the lives of the Bedouins of the Negev. The student volunteers at both Sapir College and Ben Gurion University were Bedouins from the Negev. Though they were already familiar with the area, volunteering there caused them to recognize the common difficulties and needs of the Bedouin communities. The students reported that the activism and group encounters with other volunteers were experiences that gave them a sense of belonging in their home settings as well as in the larger Bedouin community.

"I am no more Rassem from Tel Sheva," said one of the graduates, "I am Rassem of the Naqeb."

There are at least three explanations for why the Palestinian students felt they contributed and benefitted more. First, the integration of theoretical study with social engagement enriches the Palestinian students' university experience by connecting them with other Palestinian and Israeli student activists on a campus on which they felt excluded. Second, volunteering allowed them to get to know the local Palestinian community and made them feel more connected to the locale of their campus. Third, even though most of the Palestinian students are only permitted to get Perah scholarships for tutoring individual children, they—the privileged minority of the Arab minority—perceived their work with the less privileged Palestinian community as activism in the name of solidarity and social change.

The finding that Palestinian students felt their social involvement was enriching and meaningful, both for them and for the community, has an impor-tance far beyond higher education and civic engagement. Since the establish-ment of the state of Israel, all Jewish youth are conscripted into the military at age 18. Arabs are not asked to do the same, nor could they have complied with such a request. The majority of Arab youth also do not take part in "national service," which was initially designed for Jewish religious girls who do not want to serve in the army but want to contribute in a different way. Since national service is budgeted and led by the Ministry of Defense and regarded by the

View from Lion's Gate cemetery

Arab community as linked to the army, they prefer not to be part of it. There are many scholarships and social benefits reserved for people who served in the army or did national service and are not available to Palestinians.

Community-Engaged Courses

Research from all over the world has indicated the importance of faculty involvement in processes of student civic engagement through courses that integrate theory and practice. Students affirm that involvement on the part of their teachers deepened their engagement with the community and that class discussions enabled them to cope with questions and issues that arose during their work in the field.[25] The role of the lecturer is different in community-engaged courses: rather than purveyors of knowledge, teachers become stewards of learning. They, too, learn from their students and from the organizations and communities they work with.[26]

Frequently, lecturers see community-engaged courses as a means of enhancing student comprehension and providing them with professional experience. The tangible results of community activism are considered secondary. Hence, scholars suggest that in order to develop partnerships that are meaningful for all sides it is essential to stress the importance of forming bonds with the community, build trust, and developing long-term commitment.[27]

Qualitative research conducted by the Zofnat Institute examined eleven of the community-engaged courses developed by the Campus-Community Partnership in eight institutions of higher education in Israel. One of the findings was that the combination of theoretical instruction and supervision of the students' fieldwork placed a heavy workload on the lecturers.[28] This was in addition to the increasingly heavy load placed on lecturers for other reasons. Between 1973 and 2010, the number of students in Israeli higher education went up 428 percent (mainly after the colleges began to appear in the 1990s); the number of senior academic faculty increased by only 40 percent.[29] The institutions for higher education have turned to outsourcing and today most of the teachers at colleges and universities are employed as adjuncts, with no job security, under conditions that make it impossible to conduct research. These lecturers have an even harder time supervising students who are active in the field, both because of limited time resources and because this supervision—which is very time consuming and requires that they be available and attuned to their students at all times—does not carry the same weight as an academic publication.

A study I conducted with Nadera Shalhoub Kevorkian examined 13 community engaged (service-learning) courses on 11 campuses in Israel, all of them supported by the Campus-Community Partnership and all of them dealing with human rights and social justice. We found that over 80 percent of the students who participated in these courses regarded neither the activism nor the course as political or politically charged.[30] The students and the lecturers differentiated neatly between what they considered "social" and what they considered "political" and chose to engage only with the former. All the courses integrated theory and practice and gave students opportunities to discuss dilemmas, knowledge, and insights that arose during their community work. About a third of the students were Palestinians. This increased representation is indicative of both the Palestinian students' interest in the courses and the faculty's motivation and desire to facilitate an encounter between Jewish and Palestinian students to promote human rights and social change. The faculty members made it a goal to create spaces in which Jewish and Arab students could engage in meaningful dialogue about their social activism on behalf of human rights.

There were four main findings. First, all of the students who participated in the study concluded that the integration of theory and practice was the most effective learning modality and expressed their eagerness to participate in more courses of this nature.

Second, Palestinian students in general, and Palestinian women in particular, stressed the importance of, and an urgent need for, a safe space in which they could speak freely on campus. One Palestinian female student stated, "In class, I realized that it is safe to share, cooperate, create, [there was] an appropriate atmosphere that maintained mutual respect."

The issue of mutual respect and the ability to share without fear was of utmost concern to Palestinian students. One woman explained:

The most important thing that happened in class was that I was able to speak my mind without fear. I felt safe in sharing my ideas and my own analyses, with no threat.

Many students reported in interviews that the partnership classroom was the only place on campus where they sensed mutual respect and a rare opportunity to share their personal experiences with Jewish students.

Third, for most of the Arab and Jewish students, the course constitutes their first opportunity to encounter one another. Most students elaborated on the importance of meeting the "other" and regretted the dearth of such opportunities on campus and in Israeli society in general. One of the students wrote: "The discussions were the most important thing in the class, with friends from the Jewish and Arab sectors addressing problems and their solutions. There was a lot of action because everyone had an opinion and it was very interesting to listen and participate."

Students stated that participating in these courses allowed them to go beyond the boundaries of their own identity and negotiate with, learn about, and contribute to, the larger social good.

One female Palestinian student stated:

> This is the first time I'm participating in a course that combines members from both communities [Jewish and Palestinian]. I see the challenge here. I see it because I want to know the other group a bit more, I want to have contact with them, I want to learn their language, to understand them.

Her voice, as well as that of many students continually referred to the otherness of the other group, while searching for commonalities rather than differences:

> I met women from other groups and classes. I listened to them, learned to know them more closely, internalized that every human being is different, and we are similar in some issues and different in others (Palestinian female).

> I participated in many meetings between Arabs and Jews. They always brought leftist Jews and very leftist Arabs to the meeting, and it was like convincing the convinced. I believe that in our class we made a real endeavor, a sincere effort, for in our class we also have rightist Arabs and Jews.

Hence, the fact that the Partnership-sponsored courses are regular academic courses taking place at academic institutions across Israel, and are open to all students on campus and not only to those who chose to participate in "Peace Education" programs, appears to have turned such new contacts, discussions, learning, and border-crossings into a more authentic collective first step. One clear finding is that both Palestinian and Jewish students were actively engaged in building a community of students aimed at pursuing a more just, equitable society. As one male Palestinian student explained:

> I think the course constructed a group that could bridge social and ideological gaps. The fact that we all worked together to achieve one goal created a sense of solidarity that could never have been achieved in other settings.

The fourth finding was that students perceive, and are invested in, the depoliticization of the campus or in their own words "leaving politics outside of the classroom." Despite the importance of raising awareness of taboo issues such as discriminatory policy in planning and housing, or discrimination between Jewish and Palestinian students, or between women and men, students preferred to avoid talking about what they perceived as "politics."

They understood the word in a narrow sense, associating it only with the Israeli–Palestinian conflict. Both faculty and students avoided explicit discussion of this topic in class. For example, the question "What troubles you about your world?" elicited many answers, but only 10 of 282 students who responded to the questionnaire mentioned the Israeli–Palestinian conflict and only four mentioned the military occupation of the West Bank and Gaza. The word "peace" appeared only 10 times—not always in positive contexts. When asked about their motivation for registering for the course, the only two students who cited their desire to learn more about the political situation were the two foreign participants. Both of them were students in Bezalel's informal architecture program. Most of the students were Israeli; the lead faculty member was Palestinian and his associate was Israeli. The students worked with a small Palestinian community in East Jerusalem to plan a public school in an area that has not had any municipal planning since 1967. None of the students, with the exception of the two foreign students, regarded the course as political. When asked at the end of the year whether the political situation had impacted their social involvement, one student in this course wrote: "Sometimes, the situation prevented us from getting to the neighborhood and prevented the residents from getting to us."

The vast majority of students in all other courses, both Israeli and Palestinian (almost 80 percent) said the question was irrelevant because the political situation was not germane to their activism. They perceived their activism as apolitical and drew a clear distinction between it and the conflict. The discussion of Israel inside the Green Line was considered one of social justice, democracy and human rights and not "politics"—though these are decidedly political issues. The discussion of what is going on "over there," beyond the Green Line in the Palestinian Occupied Territories, is regarded as political. Students preferred to discuss the difficulties, pain, and inequality within Israel and not beyond the Green Line. They wanted to work for justice close to home, support at-risk youth, and help NGOs build projects in their home communities. They left the questions of war and peace and the Israeli–Palestinian conflict off campus.

At the end of the year, most participants tended to use professional language without making reference to political opinion. Students from gender studies wrote about the importance of gender sensitivity, the community interpreting students wrote about language barriers, law students outlined the difficulties in implementation of the law and argued that if the legal system was more accessible and fairer to certain social groups, inequality could be significantly reduced. Likewise, urban planners used professional terms pertaining to space in order to describe the situations they had studied.

Several factors prevented the students from discussing the politics of the Israeli–Palestinian conflict and the military occupation of the Palestinian territories. The first is related to the sense of hopelessness that prevails in this regard. Like most Israelis and Palestinians, lecturers and students feel despair, weariness, apathy, and lack of faith in a potential resolution. This attitude often manifests in a lack of interest in the conflict and focus on alternative social causes that are less controversial. This is true of the popular protest movement that emerged in 2011, which focused on social justice and completely ignored how the political situation affects the economy and society. Palestinian students had talked about their despair: One Palestinian female student stated, "We live and breathe injustices [...] this country was built on injustice. We just need to forget [...] to live."

Students also avoided discussing the conflict because they valued the group and did not want to create tensions in it. In interviews, students confessed that they believed discussion of difficult political topics might jeopardize the safe space that had been created in the classroom. They relied on the group support and the friendships that emerged were valuable to them. They feared losing these by way of political discourse.

Another explanation for the absence of political discourse in the classroom is fear. Palestinian students reported that they were afraid to express political views that were considered illegitimate in the hegemonic Israeli discourse, including on campus.

The walls have ears [...] So, we study, we promote ourselves and societies, we make friends, meet teachers, intellectuals [...]. But we are kept in prison, for, as our parents were told in 1948 and as we were raised to remember, the walls have ears.

Another female Palestinian student explained in an interview:

You could talk about what can be talked about. Issues that should not be talked about are not talked about [illi ma binhaka [...] ma binhakash [...] wala bitnaqash].

The position demonstrated here might reflect a culture of fear in academia, one that undermines so-called academic freedom. In the interviews, some students said that they preferred to focus on their personal struggles, as the price of challenging the political system might be too taxing.

Research on the Israeli education system affirms these feelings. Scholars argue that control over curricula and incentivizing appointment of teachers and principals who are approved by the security services were in effect a screening for political activists or those perceived as likely to act on behalf of the rights of Palestinians in Israel as a minority in their homeland. The monitoring of the education system included the planting of collaborators in the system itself. Thus, the reality of both overt and covert surveillance affected Palestinians' ability to speak, organize, write, and resist discriminatory policies and ideologies.[31]

In comparison with elementary and secondary schools, where curricula and the personal backgrounds of teachers and principals are monitored, the higher education system has more freedom. Nevertheless, there are limits to the freedom of expression and protest that students who oppose certain Israeli policies have on the campuses.

This position is indicative of a culture of fear that undermines the prevailing view that the campuses offer academic freedom. Some of the students explained that they preferred to focus on their personal struggles because they feared that if they provoked the political system, they would pay a heavy price. A Palestinian student from the Technion described her choice to avoid expressing her opinions about the conflict thus:

> I never talk to my fellow students. I never express my opinion of what they say or the standard jokes they tell about Arabs. I keep quiet. Once I responded and expressed an opinion and they ostracized me for five years. But I'll get over it. This isn't the place for arguments.

The students are not alone in this caution and sense of isolation—lecturers experience them too. It is important to note that in recent years there have been severe curtailments of academic freedom in Israel, as well as of Palestinian rights and the activities of NGOs. The Israeli Academic Monitor and the neo-fascist Im Tirzu are organizations that aim to monitor, censor, and control the content of academic courses. Moreover, they pressure foreign donors to make the transfer of funds contingent on certain faculty members keeping with the consensus or being fired.

The lecturers who participated in the study described an atmosphere of fear, silencing, and self-censorship on campus. One of them noted that academic institutions treat the Partnership as an "intrusive foreign body" or a "stepchild." She said, "We feel paralyzed and compelled to self-censor. We know what is allowed and what isn't."

The findings of this study affirm previous claims apropos the attempt to depoliticize Israeli academia and the avoidance of teaching topics such as the Israeli occupation of Palestinian territories.[32] Moreover, it warrants examining whether this situation is perpetuated by the growing numbers of students active in scholarship programs or community-engaged courses that remain avoidant of the Israeli–Palestinian conflict. As such, the resources, knowledge, and energy of these students, along with their desire to bring about change, are channeled into activism that lacks political context.

The campus forum

Chapter 6

THIS IS NOT "CO-HUMMUS"

In 2011, a regular session of the Minerva Human Rights Fellowship Program fell on Nakba day. Some of the Palestinian students gave advance notice that they would not be in attendance on this memorial to their collective tragedy. Absence is sometimes a political statement more powerful than words. In the educational interests of all the students, and to avoid having the Palestinian students miss a class, I suggested that we learn about the Nakba together. I asked Manal, one of the Palestinian students, to prepare a presentation. Manal related the story of how her grandmother's family was uprooted in 1948 from their home in Masr and how, until the day she died, Manal's grandmother yearned for the land that became the site of Kibbutz Metzer. This caused an uproar in class. Rachel commented, "I came today expecting to learn about the Nakba, but I was wrong. I expected to learn the background and not just hear a personal story. What I lack is knowledge." Adva and Yael also insisted that they were interested in the facts rather than stories. "How many people were expelled and how many fled of their own accord?" "What role did the Arab leadership play?" Dorit, on the other hand, kept repeating, "It's awful. It's really awful to hear."

The discussion grew tense and as the flood of questions directed at Manal amplified, the Palestinian students came to her assistance. Rada said, "I feel uncertain about whether I should be here or at the march, the demonstration. I don't know how much I can stand here and talk about it. It's very difficult for me. It's threatening and frightening. I'm afraid today."

The Jewish–Israeli students asked me angrily why I countenanced storytelling rather than the presentation of facts. I tried to grasp why it was so hard for them to listen to the stories and why they insisted on numbers.

In the days following that lesson, I talked with pained students, Israeli and Palestinian. They all said that this was the first opportunity they had had to discuss the Nakba with the other side. Still, when Leah apologized to Manal at the next session, I was surprised. Leah, an ultraorthodox student who lives in a settlement and was doing her internship at a rape crisis center, addressed Manal in front of the class: "What I did to Manal is exactly what I never want to be done to my patients. I poked and prodded without being mindful of your pain. I hurt you like the interrogators and detectives who ask intrusive questions hurt rape victims." Leah's apology led to a lengthy discussion about how difficult it is to listen, to inquire, and to have our worldviews challenged. "The things I am learning from my friends here go against everything we've been educated on. It's like one small earthquake after another," said Roni. "But maybe there's something positive about earthquakes in that they challenge our assumptions."

The tense conversation cycled back repeatedly to two questions: How many Palestinians were forced to leave and how many left because Arab leadership called on them to do so? And why did the Arab leaders not accept the Partition Plan of 1947?

As Stanley Cohen explained, there are different paths to denial. From literal denial (the Nakba never happened), some of the students transitioned to interpretive denial: How many hundreds of thousands of Palestinians left their homes in 1948? Did they do so of their own free will or were they expelled? Who bears responsibility for the catastrophe? Did you cause your catastrophe or did we?

Manal and Rada did not grow up in abandoned villages. Even their parents were born after the Nakba. But each one of them had a grandmother, an aunt, or a distant relative who had experienced the expulsion and who still longs for her home and land, now occupied by Jews. With courage and candor, Manal shared with her Israeli friends the pain caused by the silencing of the Palestinian story. In response, the Jewish students wanted to know how many people had lived in Masr and exactly how much land they had owned before 1948.

In the age of the internet, students have easy access to information about Lifta, Palestinian abandoned villages (including Masr), the Arab house they are renting in Jerusalem, and the past of the neighborhoods they live in. What Leah managed to understand was that for Manal and her friends, it was the experience of "trauma" and not the details that mattered. It was a delayed insight that enabled her to compare Manal speaking to the class about the Nakba to a rape victim relating the experience to the police, that is, to identify it as a revisiting of the trauma. Feminist writers observe that sexual violence, particularly within the family, is an insidious trauma; many rape survivors live in ongoing fear of the trauma being repeated. Insidious trauma is constantly relived and can result in serious post-traumatic symptoms.[1] A significant number of Palestinian students experience a comparable fear of the recurrence of trauma and hence of discussing the initial trauma. That day in class Fahed said, "I don't want there to be another Nakba. I see the situation of Palestinians in Jerusalem, Gaza and the West Bank and I don't want to see the residents of Sheikh Jarrah or Silwan turned into refugees again. I'm not optimistic. I just hope there won't be another Nakba."

For most Palestinians, the Nakba is an insidious trauma and they experience the appropriation of their lands, the conquest of Jerusalem, Gaza, and the Golan, as its direct continuation. Most Israelis, on the other hand, don't know, don't want to know, don't believe in this experience—or are not willing to acknowledge it.

The majority of Israelis, including liberals and human rights advocates, fear the repercussions of acknowledging the Nakba. They ask: "So what do you want? To return to your homes and lands? That will be the end of the state of Israel as a Jewish state."

Denial of the Palestinians' formative traumatic event by most of the Israeli public poses a difficult—perhaps insurmountable—challenge. It places the burden of educating Israelis on the Palestinian students and, so, forces them to relive the trauma. This makes encounters between Israeli and Palestinian students more and more difficult as the disparities between their worldviews grow wider. Given the inherent inequality between Israelis and Palestinians, it is unfair to ask the Palestinian student minority, which feels foreign and threatened, to share its experiences with the Israeli students so that the latter can learn about what they don't want to know, and what has been deliberately hidden from them for decades. As I have demonstrated, it's not just the Nakba that is denied on campus and throughout the education system. The occupation is absent from the educational discourse.

In recent decades Jewish-Arab/Palestinian dialogue programs (which are geared mostly toward high school students) have come under severe criticism in Israel.[2] Most scholars concur that these programs have had a negligible long-term impact on the participants' views. They have also failed to effect a positive influence on wider circles, beyond the participants themselves, that is, there was no evidence of impact on the home communities of the participants.

Scholars have identified the disadvantages of dialogue programs, explaining their failure to exert long-term influence on how Israelis and Palestinians view each other. First, such programs are typically one-time events lasting several days. In the absence of long-term exposure, their influence fades rapidly.[3] Second, these meetings usually occur at a remove from the everyday lives of the participants and disconnected from the ongoing violence affecting their lives. This makes the participants feel that the meetings are artificial and contrived.[4] Third, many of the encounters focus on the cultural and interpersonal aspects of identity while neglecting, sometimes intentionally, social and political issues. The conflict is thus reduced to the interpersonal, blurring the deep structures and institutional mechanisms that perpetuate inequality between the two groups.[5] Fourth, researchers investigating these dialogue events in Israel tend to overlook the fact that their effect on Arabs and Jews, given their unequal positions in the dialogue, is not the same. Fifth, for the most part, participants in dialogue groups volunteer to do so, while opponents of peace and reconciliation avoid such forums. And finally, there are very few efforts to follow up. The participants are hence left without tools to link the one-time event to their everyday lives and the lessons learned are not implemented in reality.

In contrast to the short-term nature of dialogue meetings, community-engaged academic courses such as the Minerva Human Rights Fellows Program lasts an entire year. The course enables Israeli and Palestinian to meet in an academic environment and learn together. Because everyone is involved in social justice and human rights activism, the focus is on their attempts to bring about change.

At the start of the 2016–2017 school year, I asked the students my customary question about a sense of injustice they had experienced in the near or distant past. Bassima responded:

It happened this morning. I just wanted to sit on the bus. I didn't want to get off, wait, cross the checkpoint on foot and take another bus on the other side. I just wanted to sit with the internationals who stayed seated and were going to cross the checkpoint on the bus. This is not the first time I've come from Ramallah in the morning. I'm from Jerusalem and I know the checkpoint. But this morning I was tired and I just sat there. And then a soldier came and yelled at me to get off, saying that I know I'm not allowed to stay on the bus. I got off.

Bassima spoke quietly in tentative Hebrew. Wearing a hijab and elegant makeup, she sat in her chair and demonstrated how she had leaned back into the bus seat that she had not wanted to vacate. She did not tell the class about her fiancé who had been in prison for months. Neither, in the months that followed, did she tell them that he was given a two-year sentence. She did not talk about the times her 15-year-old brother was arrested, nor about her father being released from prison. She did not share this with the 10 Jewish students in the class, but the other Palestinian students all knew. Right from the beginning of the year, they knew that the story she told was only a small part of the harsh occupation reality she had to contend with. Most Palestinian students opt for this sharing of snippets because they fear being exposed.

Every year, at the end of the program, students attest to the importance of the shared meals and mutually enlightening interactions, characterizing them as formative and life-changing. Many speak of major shifts: "I'm not the same person I was at the beginning of the year. My awareness, my consciousness, has changed." Jewish students speak about seeing Jerusalem in a different light and about how the encounter with Palestinian students is the most significant experience of their academic careers. Palestinian students speak about the tools they have acquired and how much they learned from the discussion with the Israelis.

Over the years, group tours of Jerusalem have become almost impossible because the Palestinian students do not want to be seen off campus with the Israeli students. In the spring of 2017, we toured Silwan with Emek Shaveh, an Israeli organization of archeologists dedicated to preventing the politicization of archaeology in the context of the Israeli–Palestinian conflict. Their main focus is on the City of David—an archeological site of the extreme right-wing organization ELAD, which is visited each year by about half a million Israelis. The site's archeological findings are controversial, erasing hundreds of years of history to prove that Jerusalem was King David's city. We saw the settlers' houses built in the middle of the village that is home to more than fifty thousand Palestinians who are consistently denied building rights. The Palestinian students felt uncomfortable on the tour and so they split off into a separate group. Ennass explained:

How can I expect a Palestinian whose house and lands have been taken over by the Jewish settlers to establish the City of David to understand what I and the other Palestinian students are doing with a group of Israelis inside the settlement? This feeling is not just for fear of what they'll say about us if they see us in this context, but about the fact that we, as Palestinians, want to learn about our land and history and the situation of the residents of Silwan from the villagers themselves. Who better than they, know and have experienced the occupation? We don't want to learn this reality from Israelis.

Hala Marshood, my teaching assistant, proposed a separate tour as soon as she noticed the discomfort. It was a good solution for that day, albeit a sad one. Rada concluded her feedback on the tour with these words:

The tour exposed me and the other Palestinian students to ideas and questions that most of us would never encounter if we had continued to discuss the settlements only inside the Hebrew University or in some other safe and removed space. Eventually, like anything else in life, getting to know something first hand, far from the academy and books, even though it is difficult and complicated, is the best way to understand what's being addressed and how to work towards changing it. As long as we are removed from reality we will never work to change or fix things with conviction, understanding, and collegiality.

At the end of the year, Ennass told her classmates that the tour taken as part of this course was her first visit to Silwan. "I was born and raised and still live walking distance from Silwan," she said. "The first time I walked through this neighboring village and talked to its people was with a Hebrew University group."

Food

When I think of the students it has been my privilege to teach, I think of food. One example is the kosher chicken—made unkosher because it was stuffed with kosher cheese—that Ramzi prepared with love, and the ensuing conversation about kashrut that followed. The separation of meat and dairy is obvious to Jews in Israel. In the campus cafeterias, the separation between the milk side and the meat side is strict. Ramzi, who grew up in East Jerusalem, knew that there was kosher chicken and made a special trip to the mall in the heart of West Jerusalem to buy kosher chicken and kosher cheese, which he combined into a beautiful dish. Kosher food unified Jewish communities in the diaspora, setting them apart from others. It is still unusual for Jews and Arabs to eat together. There were three vegetarians in the class, two vegans and one ultraorthodox Jew. Ramzi had never heard of the fact that kashrut prohibits the mixing of dairy and meat. Luckily, he also brought six different excellent salads. The discussion of vegan, vegetarian, kosher and ultra-kosher food, was accompanied by tea drinking in glass cups. The conversation and the attempts to translate vegan terms into Arabic nourished us all.

The shared meal defined us as a group and forced all the students, Jews and Arabs, to eat together for the first time in their lives. It also gave them the opportunity to discuss their place in the group and their feelings. In good years we were lucky enough to enjoy stuffed vine leaves prepared by Rania's mother, *meluchia* cooked by Ahmed's mother, and the vegan *maklubah* cooked by Meital's mother. We have enjoyed Irit's four cheese and spinach quiches and Leo's lasagna. The food featured prominently in the end-of-year feedback. When I asked a student named Mor Efrat what she remembered most, she answered, "It was the only place on campus I felt that I could speak. I also remember the lemon mousse I made." I, too, can still taste her lemon mousse and her outstanding chocolate cake.

The meal helped the Israeli and Palestinian students to talk, to breathe, and to bond. It was the key to consolidating us as a group and it made the double lesson an anticipated event. Students are always hungry. In a four-hour lesson that often involved tough conversations, food was a comfort. Sometimes, the divisive reality challenged us to think and talk about food, and the place in which we were eating it, as a metaphor for the greater conflict in which we are mired.

I've always been conscious of the role that food plays in societies living in conflict, particularly in the colonial context. In my book *Next Year in Jerusalem*, I devote an entire chapter to the absence of food at meetings between the Israeli and Palestinian women's organization that I codirected—"the Jerusalem Link."[6] The reluctance to eat together symbolized the disparity between us, the Israelis who wanted to have fun, eat together and believe that friendly relations are possible, and the Palestinian women who like most Palestinian organizations, did not want to "normalize relations" with Israelis.

In the years I have taught the human rights fellowship and other community-engaged courses, I have come to understand how important it is for young people to talk and get to know one another and how few are their opportunities to do so. Given the violent, ongoing conflict between Israelis and Palestinians, and the worsening enmity, the campus is the only possible venue for dialogue and fostering of interactions between Arabs and Jews. Attention, openness to different voices, and food—all these benefit the encounter. Respectful discourse, on any subject, even food, can ignite processes of change. For example, Mizrahi students moved during the academic year from total denial and resistance ("I grew up in Ashdod and not one of my cousins is interested in university. That's why there are no Mizrahi academics") to recognition of the institutionalized discrimination against their parents and grandparents who originated in Arab countries. The meeting with Arab students over food allowed them to taste the nearness of the past. "My grandmother makes *maklubah* like this. I never wanted her to speak Arabic to me. Now I hear Arabic in class and I am sorry," remarked one of the Mizrahi students.

Food is, of course, a political subject. In 1957, Albert Memmi published *The Colonizer and the Colonized*, which dealt with the French occupation of Tunis. He wrote about the colonizer:

Having first eaten couscous with curiosity, he now tastes it from time to time out of politeness and finds that "it's filling, it's degrading and it's not nourishing." It is "torture by suffocation," he says humorously. Or, if he does like couscous, he cannot stand that "fairground music" which seizes and deafens him each time he passes a café. "Why so loud? How can they hear each other?"[7]

On the one hand, Israelis relate to indigenous Palestinian cuisine with an orientalist interest in finding the most authentic Palestinian hummus. Israelis appropriate hummus-falafel as their national dish. Hummus and falafel are local, cheap, unpretentious, suitable for the local climate and beloved by most Israelis.[8] Mass-produced kosher hummus is one of the best-selling products in Israel, including to Palestinian consumers. Furthermore, the mythos of hummus epitomizes the Israeli fantasy of coexistence. This attitude of "we'll sit, share some hummus and everything will be ok," is referred to as "co-hummus," that is, a coexistence that ignores the power relations, discrimination and fear for the future that prevail. Palestinians recoil from the Israeli colonial-orientalist proposal to "sharing some hummus." In recent years, the Israeli presence in Palestinian restaurants has declined and most Palestinians do not want to be seen with Israelis in these restaurants, or in any other Palestinian space.

"At the beginning of the year, I did not want to talk to you Israelis. I certainly didn't want to be your friend," were Samar's words at the end of the academic year in the summer of 2017. "We came to study, not to talk. But little by little I got more and more familiar. During the year I went home and told my father that there are Israelis who you can talk to. He said it was impossible." Samar brought delicious sweets from her father's bakery to the meeting. His bakery is one of the best known in the old city and the few still frequented by some Israelis. "My father still does not believe that there are Israelis who feel our pain, the pain of the Palestinians," said Samar. "The shared meals were a comfort to me. There were days when the food was almost the only comfort."

At the beginning of January 2009, on a day when we'd planned to visit schools in East Jerusalem close to the campus, the Gaza war, known as "Operation Cast Lead," broke out. Our plan to learn about crowded and insufficient classrooms, and the resulting thousands of Palestinian children who have no place in schools, morphed into a walking tour of Ein Karem. We walked in silence and then sat down in a dairy Italian restaurant in an Arab house to discuss the war in Gaza. It had just begun and we were all alarmed, angry, and afraid. Both Jews and Arabs said this was the first time that they had discussed the war with the other. Many said this was the first time they had discussed the war with anyone outside their families. Amani said, "All I could think about during the walk was the refugees. They were present all the time. The food in the restaurant was tasty but the conversation was harsh." The conversation in the restaurant had lasted three hours, with intermittent smoke breaks outdoors. On the sidewalk outside that restaurant, we cried. We talked and cried; we ate and drank; we felt relieved that we were still a group.

I admit that a kosher Italian restaurant in Ein Karem was a strange choice for a group of Arab and Jewish students. It was, however, not coincidental. Moran, my teaching assistant, and I deliberated the night before regarding the choice of venue. East Jerusalem was besieged by police, making our visit to the schools impossible. Ein Karem, on the other hand, was close enough to campus but also far enough inside West Jerusalem to feel safe. I know a magical, little-known, trail through the hills. The walk enabled us to spend half an hour in nature, among the olive trees with views of the hills and churches. We walked in silence, lost in thought. Most of the students, both Jews and Arabs, were unaware that Ein Karem was once a Palestinian village. Most of the Jewish students also did not know that hundreds of thousands of refugees that now live in Gaza once lived in villages just like this one.

Today, the tension in Jerusalem is so extreme that it would be unlikely to find Jews and Palestinians sitting in a restaurant together. But in a class on Mount Scopus, if the conflict, the inequality, the occupation, the Nakba, and our war-torn history can be acknowledged, hope is still on the table. The shared meal gives one an appetite for more; there is comfort in that.

View from Mount Scopus

NOTES

Introduction

1 Al Aqsa intifada also known as the second Palestinian uprising started in September 2000, after Ariel Sharon provocatively visited the Temple Mount.

2 Daphna Golan, " Then I Said the Word 'Occupation,' " *Haaretz*, June 15, 2017. https://www.haaretz.co.il/opinions/.premium-1.4176051. [Hebrew]

3 Daphna Golan-Agnon, *Next Year in Jerusalem: Everyday Life in a Divided Land* (New York: New Press, 2005).

4 *Voices from Sheikh Jarrah*. The Hebrew University and Bezalel, 2010.

1 The Mount Scopus Campus

1 Shmuel Yosef Agnon, *Shira*, ed. Robert Alter, trans. Zeva Shapiro (New York: Toby Press, 2013).

2 Stanley Cohen, "The Virtual Reality of Universities in Israel," in *A Time to Speak Out: Independent Jewish Voices on Israel, Zionism and Jewish Identity*, ed. Anne Kapf, Brian Klug, Jacqueline Rose, Barbara Rosenbaum (London: Verso, 2008), 36–46 http://archive.jpr.org.uk/object-uk90.

3 Moshe Ehrnvald, *A Siege within a Siege: Mount Scopus during the War of Independence* (Jerusalem: Yad Yitshak Ben-Tsevi, 2010). [Hebrew]

4 Ibid., 15.

5 Meron Benvenisty, *City of Stone* (Berkeley: University of California Press, 1998), 23–30.

6 Minutes of the Standing Committee of the Senate, June 11, 1967. Hebrew University Archives. Sixty-five committee members voted in favor and four abstained, in Guy Yadin Evron, "The Return; Nathan Rotenstreich, the Hebrew University and East Jerusalem," Unpublished seminar paper, [Hebrew] Hebrew University of Jerusalem, 2017.

7 Ibid.

8 The *dunam* is a measure of land area used in parts of the former Ottoman Empire, including Israel (where it is equal to 1,000 square meters—about a quarter of an acre).

9 Yacobi Haim. "Academic Fortress: The Planning of the Hebrew University Campus on Mount Scopus," in *Urban Universities and Development: The International Experience*, ed. D. Perry and W. Wiewel (Cambridge: Lincoln Institute of Land Policy, 2008), pp. 257–72.

10   "Discussion summary" Israel Land Authority, December 11, 1969, in Evron, "The Return."

11   David Kroyanker, *Architecture in Jerusalem: Modern Construction beyond the City Walls, 1948–1990*, vol. 5 (Jerusalem: Keter, 1991), 132.

12   Nir Hasson, *URSHALIM: Israelis and Palestinians in Jerusalem, 1967–2017* (Tel Aviv: Sifre 'aliyat ha-Gag, 2017), 51. [Hebrew]

13   Dianna Dolev, "Hebrew University Architectural Master Plans 1918–1948," in *The History of the Hebrew University of Jerusalem: Origins and Beginnings*, ed. Shaul Katz and Michael Heyd (Jerusalem: Magnes Press, 1997), 257–80. Ayala Levin writes about the campus designers' notion of building a modern city surrounded by a wall with a tower at its center, overlooking the Old City—with classrooms-like shops and hallways like the streets. Ayala Levin, "The Mountain and the Fortress: The Location of the Hebrew University Campus on Mount Scopus in the Israeli Imagination of National Space," *Theory and Criticism* 38/39 (Winter 2011): 11–34. [Hebrew]

14   Dianna Dolev, "Architecture, Education and Power: A Feminist Perspective on the University Campus," in *Militarism in Education*, ed. Haggith Gor Ziv (Tel Aviv: Bavel, 2005), 187–203. [Hebrew]

15   Ibid., 191.

16   Gayil Har'even, *Ani Leona* (Tel Aviv: Ahuzath Bayit, 2014), 374.

17   Michal Frenkel, "Things You Cannot Say in Class," *Pickpook*, February 17, 2014. http://www.pickpook.org/2014/02/page/2/. [Hebrew]

18   Ibid.

19   Stanley Cohen, *States of Denial: Knowing about Atrocities and Suffering* (London: Polity, 2001).

20   Ibid., x.

21   Stanley Cohen and Daphna Golan. *The Interrogation of Palestinians during the Intifada* (Jerusalem: B'Tselem, The Israeli Information Center for Human Rights in the Occupied Territories, 1991). https://www.btselem.org/publications/summaries/199103_torture.

22   Stanley Cohen, "Human Rights and Crimes of the State: The Culture of Denial," *Australian and New Zealand Journal of Criminology* 26, no. 2 (1993): 97–115. John Barry Memorial Lecture, University of Melbourne, September 30, 1992, 101.

23   Judith Lewis Herman, *Trauma and Recovery: The Aftermath of Violence: From Domestic Abuse to Political Terror* (New York: Basic Books, 2015), 25.

24   Yehouda Shenhav, "The Sociologists and the Occupation," *Israeli Sociology* 9, no. 2 (2008): 263–70. [Hebrew]

25   Or Kashti, "Israeli University Rebukes Professor Who Expressed Sympathy for Both Israeli, Gazan Victims," *Haaretz*. N.p., July 29, 2014. November 1, 2016. http://www.haaretz.com/israel-news/.premium-1.607888.

26   Gidi Weitz, "Signs of Fascism in Israel Reached New Peak during Gaza Op, Says Renowned Scholar," *Haaretz*. N.p., August 13, 2014. https://www.haaretz.com/.premium-signs-of-fascism-in-israel-peaked-during-gaza-op-1.5259272.

27   The last sentence was published only in the Hebrew (original) version of the article—not in the English one.

28   "The Thirteenth Council for Higher Education: Policy Decisions 2007–2012," 16. http://che.org.il/wp-content/uploads/2012.

2 Issawiyye: Palestinian Citizens of Israel (Students) Encounter Palestinian Youth Living under the Occupation

1 Uri Agnon, "Looking Down at Issawiyye from the Mount," *Haoketz*, March 31, 2016. [Hebrew] First presented at the conference *The Campus and the Village: Studying the Humanities facing Issawiyye*, The Hebrew University, March 27, 2016.

2 Nir Hasson, "Israel's Parks Authority Names Plan to Demolish Palestinian Structures 'They See Not, Nor Know,'" *Haaretz*,
  November 13, 2012. October 5, 2016. http://www.haaretz.com/israel-news/israel-s-parks-authority-names-plan-to-demolish-palestinian-structures-they-see-not-nor-know.premium-1.477499. The words "They See Not, Nor Know" come up twice in the Bible. They appear in Isaiah 44:9: "they see not, nor know; that they may be ashamed" and in Psalms 82:5: "They know not, neither will they understand; they walk on in darkness: all the foundations of the earth are out of course" (King James Bible). In both cases, the phrase is used to criticize idol worshippers and people who do not acknowledge the Jewish God.

3 Jack Khoury, "Israel Release Palestinian Hunger Striker Samer Issawi," *Haaretz*. December 23, 2013. October 6, 2016. http://www.haaretz.com/israel-news/.premium-1.565031. Gil'ad Shalit was a soldier of the Israel Defense Forces (IDF) who on June 25, 2006, was captured by Hamas militants in a cross-border raid via tunnels near the Israeli border. Hamas held him captive for over five years in Gaza, until his release on October 18, 2011, as part of a prisoner exchange deal.

4 Sana Khasheiboun, "The Meaning of Home and the Impact of Its Loss on the Palestinian Family in East Jerusalem." PhD Dissertation. The Hebrew University, Jerusalem: 2013. [Hebrew]

5 Out of the 2,230 dunams (some 550 acres), which were left to Issawiyye's residents, only a small area is left for construction: 74.4 dunams (some 15 acres) are earmarked for the expansion of the Hebrew University and 639 dunams (some 14.1 acres) are set aside for the Mount Scopus Slopes Park. This information was taken from Bimkom's website http://bimkom.org/.

6 The National Insurance Institute (2015), "The Dimensions of Poverty and Social Gaps," accessed on 2016. https://www.btl.gov.il/Publications/oni_report/Documents/oni2015.pdf. [(Hebrew)]

7 From Dr. Khasheiboun's remarks at the Minerva Human Rights Fellows course on March 1, 2014, at the Hebrew University, Jerusalem.

8 André Brink, *A Dry White Season* (London: Vintage, 1998).

9 I use pseudonyms unless I have asked and received explicit permission to use the person's first and last name in this text.

10 The "Triangle" (*al-Muthallath*) is a concentration of Arab towns and villages adjacent to the Green Line, in Israel around Wadi Ara, in which some 300,000 Palestinians citizens of Israel live.

11 Oshrat Maimon and Aviv Tatarsky, "Chamesh Shanim Avru Chalfu Mizman: Five Years Have Long since Passed … The Education System in East Jerusalem between a Rock and a Hard Place: Between Extreme Neglect and Forced Attempts—Yearly Report." Rep. Ir Amim, August 30, 2016. November 22, 2016.

http://www.iramim.org.il/sites/default/files/%D7%93%D7%95%D7%97%20%D7%97%D7%99%D7%A0%D7%95%D7%9A%201.9.2016.pdf. [Hebrew]

12   Rema Hammami, "Gendered Youth/Occupied Lives: Attitudes and Experiences of Palestinian Male and Female Youth in West Bank, Gaza Strip and Arab Jerusalem," *Analytical Report 1* (Gender and Region) (Birzeit: The Institute of Women's Studies, 2013).

13   In 2019, out of the 20,5000 students at Hebrew University 1,636 were Palestinian citizens of Israel, and 815 Palestinians residents of East Jerusalem. The number of Palestinian students from East Jerusalem at the Hebrew University grew from 154 in 2009 to 815 in 2019. Israel Central Bureau of Statistics, 2019.

14   Over twenty thousand students mentor children as big brothers/sisters in a national program that gives them scholarships worth about half their annual tuition ($ 1,500 per year). In Jerusalem, there are 3,200 Perah mentors, 400 of them Palestinians. Some forty Palestinian students mentor children in the village of Issawiyye.

15   Paulo Freire, *Pedagogy of the Oppressed* (London: Penguin Group, 1972).

16   Limor Goldner and Daphna Golan-Agnon, "The Long-term Effects of Youth Mentoring on Students Mentors' Civic Engagement Attitudes and Behavior," *Journal of Community Psychology* 45, no. 6 (2017): 691–703; Goldner, Limor and Daphna Golan, "What Is Meaningful Civic Engagement for Students? Recollections of Jewish and Palestinian Graduates in Israel," *Studies in Higher Education* 44, no. 11 (2019). https://www.tandfonline.com/doi/full/10.1080/03075079.2018.1471673

17   Janet L. Abu-Lughod, "The Demographic Transformation of Palestine," in *The Transformation of Palestine: Essays on the Origin and Development of the Arab-Israeli Conflict*, ed. Ibrahim A. Abu-Lughod (Northwestern University Press, 1987), 139–63; Nadim N. Rouhana, *Palestinian Citizens in an Ethnic Jewish State: Identities in Conflict* (New Haven: Yale University Press, 1999).

18   According to National Insurance data from 2016, 52 percent of Palestinian citizens of Israel live under the poverty line.

19   Council for Higher Education. Data for the Academic year 2017–18.

20   According to the spokesperson of the Hebrew University in September 2017.

21   In 2013, the University of Haifa announced that, for the first time, it would recognize three Muslim and Christian holidays. The Hebrew University followed suit in 2015.

22   Daphna Golan, *Inequality in Education* (Tel Aviv: Babel, 2004). [Hebrew]

23   Daphna Golan-Agnon, "Separate but Not Equal: Discrimination against Palestinian Arab Students in Israel," *American Behavioral Scientist* 49, no. 8 (2006): 1075–84.

24   Ministry of Education, Education in Numbers—2018.

25   Annual report of the National Institute for Testing and Evaluation, 2013. https://www.nite.org.il/index.php/he/research-conferences/statistics/graphs-2013.html.

26   Carol Gilligan, *In a Different Voice: Psychological Theory and Women's Development* (Cambridge: Harvard University Press, 2016).

27   Ibid.

28   M. H. Amara, "Hebrew and English Borrowings in Palestinian Arabic in Israel: A Sociolinguistic Study in Lexical Integration and Diffusion," in *Language and Society in the Middle East and North Africa—Studies in Variation and Identity*, ed. Y. Suleiman (London: Curzon Press, 1999), 81–103. See also M. H. Amara, "The Vitality of the Arabic Language in Israel from a Sociolinguistic Perspective," Adalah's Newsletter 29 (2006): 1–11.

29   Raif Zreik, "The Way Back," *Theory and Criticism* 16 (Spring 2000): 23–26. [Hebrew]
30   Yaara Saadi, Representations of the Spatial Experience of the mount Scopus Campus According to Palestinians Students. MA Thesis (Hebrew University, 2015), 3.
31   Ibid., 17–18.
32   Rabah Halabi, "Arab Students in a Hebrew University: Existing but Unnoticed." *Intercultural Education* 27, no. 6 (2016): 560–76.

3 Sheikh Jarrah: Queer Theory and the Nature of Law

1   Rema Hammami, "Home and Exile in East Jerusalem," in *Seeking Palestine: New Palestinian Writing on Exile and Home*, ed. Penny Johnson and Raja Shehadeh (Ithaca: Olive Branch Press, 2013), 111–33.
2   Michael Ben Ari, at the Minerva Center for Human Rights at the Hebrew University of Jerusalem, December 17, 2014.
3   Ibid.
4   Alon Harel, "Sheikh Jarrah as an Example," *Haaretz*, May 19, 2013.
5   Stanley Cohen, "The Human Rights Movement in Israel and South Africa: Some Paradoxical Comparisons," *Occasional Papers*, Jerusalem: Harry S. Truman Research Institute for the Advancement of Peace, N. 1, 1991.
6   Judith Butler, "Gender Trouble: Feminism and the Subversion of Identity," *Gender Trouble: Feminism and the Subversion of Identity* (New York: Routledge, 2015), 128–49.
7   Noam Chomsky, *Fateful Triangle: The United States, Israel, and the Palestinians* (Chicago, IL: South End Press, 1999); Raja Shehadeh, *The Third Way: A Journal for Life in the West Bank* (London: Quartet Books, 1982).
8   See the Molad website http://www.molad.org/en/.
9   Daphna Golan, "Anyone Can Drum," *Haaretz*, December 21, 2009.
10   Audre Lorde, "The Master's Tools Will Never Dismantle the Master's House," *Sister Outsider* (Berkeley: Crossing Press, 1984), 110–14.

4 Lifta: Site for Reconciliation

1   Walid Khalidi (ed.), *All That Remains: The Palestinian Villages Occupied and Depopulated by Israel in 1948* (Washington, DC: Institute for Palestine Studies, 1992).
2   Plan No. 6036—Residential Area for Lifta, see safelifta.org.
3   Khalidi, *All That Remains*.
4   There are various estimates of the number of Palestinian refugees displaced in 1948: 600,000–760,000 according to Morris; 714,150–744,150 according to Khalidi; or at least 780,000 according to Saadi; see Benny Morris, *The Birth of the Refugee and Palestinian Problem 1947–1949* (Tel Aviv: Am Oved, 1997). [Hebrew]
5   Nur Masalha (ed.), *Catastrophe Remembered: Palestine, Israel and the Internal Refugees* (London: Zed Books, 2005).
6   Today Jews make up 80 percent of the population of Israel, but only about half the population of Israel and the Occupied Territories combined. There are some 6.6 million Jews and 1.9 million Palestinian Arabs in Israel (Israel Central Bureau of Statistics, 2018) and some 4.8 million Palestinians in the West Bank and Gaza (Palestinian Central Bureau of Statistics, 2018).

7   Human rights organizations react as promptly as possible to house demolitions, land appropriation, administrative detention, torture, assassinations, sieges, uprooting of olive groves, skirmished with settlers, and so on. They try to help Palestinians in ways they have at their disposal and mediate between the Palestinians, the state, and international law. Because not every one of the human rights violations that occur in the Occupied Territories can be addressed individually, the organizations establish priorities according to their resources, specializations, the urgency of the case, frequency of occurrence and chances of success. However, almost all of them ignore the Nakba, the displacement of 1948 and the direct connection Palestinians make between this and their continued displacement. The Oudeh family, for example, left Lifta in 1948 and was not allowed to return. Like hundreds of thousands of Palestinians, the Oudehs are refugees. They live in Shuafat refugee camp and their home is slated for demolition. No Israeli human rights organization is defending their right to their Lifta home, or making the connection between that home and the current one that is going to be demolished.

8   Noga Kadman, *Erased from Space and Consciousness: Israel and the Depopulated Palestinian Villages of 1948* (Bloomington: Indiana University Press, 2015).

9   Daphna Golan, *Next Year in Jerusalem: Everyday Life in a Divided Land* (New York: New Press, 2005), chapter 1.

10   Tomer Gardi, *Stone, Paper* (Tel Aviv: Hakibbutz Hameuchad, 2011).

11   Souad Amiry, *Golda Slept Here* (Doha: Bloomsbury Qatar Foundation), 46–59.

12   M. Daum and O. Rudavsky, "The Ruins of Lifta: Where the Holocaust and the Nakba Meet," New York: English Documentary, 2019).

13   See also Tomer Gardi, Noga Kadman, and Amar Alaberi (eds.), *Omrim Yeshna Eretz (Once Upon a Land)* (Tel Aviv: Zochrot and Pardes Press, 2012), 485–88; Eitan Bronstein and Omer Agbarieh (eds.), *Zochrot et Bir Al Seba (Remembering Bir al Saba)* (Tel Aviv: Zochrot, 2006).

14   Oren Yiftachel and Sandy Kedar, "Landed Power: The Emergence of an Ethnocratic Land Regime in Israel," *Theory and Criticism* 16 (Spring 2000): 67–100. [Hebrew]

15   See, for example, Benny Morris, *The Birth of the Refugee and Palestinian Problem 1947–1949*; Benny Morris, *1948 and After: Israel and the Palestinians* (Oxford: Clarendon Press, 1994); Ilan Pappé, *The Ethnic Cleansing of Palestine* (Oxford: Oneworld Publications, 2006); Shabtai Teveth, "The Palestine Arab Refugee Problem and Its Origins," *Middle Eastern Studies* 26, no. 2 (1990): 214–49;

16   Tel Aviv Jaffa District Court, 00/1686 *Alexandroni and co. vs. Theodore Katz*; appeal456/01 *Theodore Katz vs. Alexandroni and co.* See also Pappe's book.

17   Yair Oron, *Hashoah, Hatkumah VehaNakba* (The Holocaust, the Rebirth and the Nakba) (Tel Aviv: Resling, 2013), 179–215; Manar Hassan, "Horban hair vehamilhama neged hazikaron: hamenatzhim and mnutzahim (The destruction of the city and the war on memory: the vanquishers and vanquished)," *Teoria vebikoret* (Theory and Criticism) 27, (2005): 197–207. Meron Benvenisti, *Sacred Landscape: The Buried History of the Holy Land since 1948* (Berkeley: University of California Press, 2000); Hillel Cohen, "The State of Israel versus the Palestinian Internal Refugees," in *Catastrophe Remembered*, ed. Nur Masalha (London: Zed Books, 2005), 56–72; Uri Ram, "Ways of Forgetting: Israel and the Obliterated Memory of the Palestinian Nakba," *Journal of Historical Sociology* 22, no. 3 (2009): 366–95.

18   Yehouda Shenhav, *The Time of the Green Line: A Jewish Political Essay* (Tel Aviv: Am Oved, 2010), 151. [Hebrew]

19   Eshkol Nevo, *Homesick* (Dalkey Archive Press, 2010).

20   Sara Ossietzky-Lazar, "Ikrit and Biram, the Full Story," *Coverage of the Arabs in Israel*, 10 (Givat Haviva: The Institute of Arabic Studies/Peace Research, 1993). [Hebrew]

21   Tarabut-Hithabrut, "The March of Return." http://www.tarabut.info/he/articles/article/miska-april-2010/.

22   See Independence Law bill (Amendment: Prohibition against marking Independence Day or the establishment of the state of Israel as a day of mourning), 2009.

23   Budget law amendment 40, 2011.

24   Petition #8661-03-11, Introduction, p. 3 and see paragraphs 47–52, pp. 16–17.

25   Proceedings of the interdisciplinary conference "Nofei Tarbut—The Heritage of Lifta" can be found on the website safelifta.org.

26   Yosi Yonah and Avihu Spivak, *Efshar Gam Acheret: Mitveh Lekinuna shel Medina Metukenet* (Tel Aviv: Hakibbutz Hameuchad and Kav Adom, 2012). [Hebrew]

27   *Salah, This Is Israel*, a film by Dudu Deri, Ruti Yuvak, and Doron Galezer. [Hebrew}

28   Lila Abu-Lughod and Ahmad H. Sa'di (eds.), *Nakba: Palestine, 1948, and the Claims of Memory* (New York: Columbia University Press, 2007); Nur Masalha (ed.) *Catastrophe Remembered*.

29   Daphna Golan-Agnon, *Inventing Shaka: Using History in the Construction of Zulu Nationalism* (Boulder, CO: Lynne Rienner, 1994); "Between Human Rights and Hope—What Israelis Might Learn from the Truth and Reconciliation Process in South Africa," *International Review of Victimology* 17, no. 1 (2010): 31–48.

30   There are some 6.6 million Jews and 1.9 million Palestinian Arabs in Israel (Israel Central Bureau of Statistics, 2018) and some 4.8 million Palestinians in the West Bank and Gaza (Palestinian Central Bureau of Statistics, 2018).

31   Ran Greenstein, "On Citizenship and Political Integration: Can We Learn from the Rise and Fall of the Apartheid Regime?," *Mishpat Vemimshal* (Law and Government) 10, no.1 (2006): 117–25.

32   Ibid.

33   André Brink, *A Dry White Season* (New York: William Morrow, 1980).

34   *Maids and Madams*, a film by Mira Hamermesh, 1986.

35   Daphna Golan, Zvika Orr, and Sami Ersheid, "Lifta and the Regime of Forgetting: Memory Work and Conservation," *Jerusalem Quarterly*, 54 (2013): 69–81.

5 Students Working for Change: Campus-Community Partnerships

1   Daphna Golan and Jonah Rosenfeld, "Learning from Successes of Community Engaged Courses in Israeli Academia," *Gilui Da'at*, 7 (2015): 15–38. [Hebrew]

2   Daphna Golan-Agnon, Jonah Rosenfeld, S. Ben Yossef, H. Knaneh, Y. Rosenfeld, D. Schrire, and B. Schwartz, "Student Action for Social Change: Mapping the Present to Build the Future," Paper presented at a conference of the Council of Higher Education, Jerusalem, 2005 (Jerusalem: National Academy of Sciences). [Hebrew]

3   Daphna Golan, Jonah Rosenfeld, and Zvika Orr, *Bridges of Knowledge: Campus-Community Partnerships in Israel* (Tel Aviv: Mofet, 2017). [Hebrew]

4   For example, Campus Compact 2000 or the Talloire Network consisting of hundreds of universities committed to social change.

5   John Puckett, Lee Benson, and Ira Harkavy (eds.), *Dewey's Dream: Universities and Democracies in an Age of Education Reform* (Philadelphia, PA: Temple University Press, 2007).

6   W. R. Harper, *The University and Democracy: The Trend in Higher Education* (Chicago, IL: University of Chicago Press, 1905).

7   W. Astin Alexander, "Student Involvement a Developmental Theory for Higher Education," *Journal of College Student Development* 40, no. 5 (1999): 515–18.

8   S. A. Ostrander, Democracy, "Civic Participation and the University: A Comparative Study of Civic Engagement on Five Campuses," *Nonprofit and Voluntary Sector Quarterly* 33, no. 1 (2004): 74–93.

9   J. Eyler, "Reflection: Linking Service and Learning—Linking Students and Communities", *Journal of Social Issues* 58, no. 3 (2002): 517–34; S. Marullo, and B. Edwards, "From Charity to Justice: The Potential of University-Community Collaboration for Social Change," *American Behavioral Scientist* 43, no. 5 (2000): 895–912.

10 B. Jacoby, *Civic Engagement in Higher Education: Concepts and Practices* (San Francisco, CA: Jossey-Bass, 2009).

11 Daphna Golan and N. Shalhoub-Kevorkian, "Engaged Academia in a Conflict Zone? Palestinian and Jewish Students in Israel," in *Understanding Campus-Community Partnerships in Conflict Zones: Engaging Students for Transformative Change*, ed. Dalya Yafa Markovich, Daphna Golan, and Nadera Shalhoub-Kevorkian (London: Palgrave Macmillan, 2019), 15–38.

12 Daphna Golan, and N. Shalhoub-Kevorkian, "Community-Engaged Courses in a Conflict Zone: A Case Study of the Israeli Academic Corpus," *Journal of Peace Education* 11, no. 2 (2014): 181–207.

13 Alexander W. Astin and Linda J. Sax, "How Undergraduates Are Affected by Service Participation," *Journal of College Student Development* 39, no. 3 (1998): 251–63.

14 H. T. Nelson et al., "Explicating Factors That Foster Civic Engagement among Students," *Journal of Public Affairs Education* 11, no. 4 (2005): 269–85.

15 E. Beaumont, et al., "Promoting Political Competence and Engagement in College Students: An Empirical Study," *Journal of Political Science Education* 2, no. 3 (2006): 249–70.

16 Dan W. Butin, Service-Learning in Theory and in Practice: The Future of Community Engagement in Higher Education (London: Palgrave Macmillan, 2010).

17 Limor Goldner and Daphna Golan-Agnon, "The Long-Term Effects of Youth Mentoring on Student Mentors' Civic Engagement Attitudes and Behavior," *Journal of Community Psychology* 45, no. 6 (2017): 691–703.

18 R. G. Bringle, J. A. Hatcher, and S. G. Jones (eds.), *International Service Learning: Conceptual Frameworks and Research* (Sterling: Stylus, 2011); J. Eyler, and D. E. Giles Jr., *Where's the Learning in Service-Learning?* (San Francisco: Jossey-Bass, 1999).

19 Goldner, Limor and Daphna Golan, "What Is Meaningful Civic Engagement for Students? Recollections of Jewish and Palestinian Graduates in Israel," *Studies in Higher Education* 44, no. 11 (2019). https://www.tandfonline.com/doi/full/10.1080/03075079.2018.1471673.

20 Ibid.

21 J. Eyler, "What International Service-Learning Research Can Learn from Research on Service Learning," in *International Service Learning: Conceptual Frameworks and Research*, ed. R. G. Bringle, J. A. Hatcher, and S.G. Jones (Sterling: Stylus, 2011), 225–42.

22 Shlomo Swirski, Etty Konor-Attias, Ariane Ophir, "Israel: A Social Report 2013" (Tel Aviv: Adva Center, 2014).

23 Daphna Golan-Agnon, "Why Arabs Are Discriminated against in the Israeli Education System?," in *Inequality in Education*, ed. D. Golan-Agnon (Tel Aviv: Babel, 2004), 54–73. [Hebrew]

24 L. Goldner, and Daphna Golan, "The Long-Term Effects of Youth Mentoring on Student Mentors' Civic Engagement Attitudes and Behavior," *Journal of Community Psychology*, February 2017. doi: 10.1002/jcop.

25 W. Alexander Astin, "Student Involvement: A Developmental Theory for Higher Education," *Journal of College Student Development* 40, no. 5 (1999): 515–18.

26 Elizabeth Campbell and Luke Eric Lassiter, "From Collaborative Ethnography to Collaborative Pedagogy: Reflections on the Other Side of Middletown Project and Community-University Research Partnerships," *Anthropology and Education Quarterly* 41, no. 4 (2010): 370–85.

27 Ahmed Allahwala, Susannah Bunce, Lesley Beagrie, Shauna Brail, Timothy Hawthorne, Sue levesque, Jurgen von Mahs, Brenda Spotton Visano, "Building and Sustaining Community-University Partnerships in Marginalized Urban Areas," *Journal of Geography* 112, no. 2 (2013): 43–57.

28 Israel Katz, Peleg Dor-Haim, Eyal Mazliach, and Linda Jacob, "A Study and Evaluation of Eleven Academic Courses of Campus-Community Partnership for Social Change Executive Summary," Zofnat Institute, August 2007. [Hebrew]

29 Dan Ben David (ed.), *State of the Nation Report: Society, Economy and Policy in Israel*, Jerusalem: Taub Center for Social Policy Studies in Israel (2013), 276 [Hebrew]

30 Daphna Golan, and Nadera Shalhoub-Kevorkian, "Community-Engaged Courses in a Conflict Zone: A Case Study of the Israeli Academic Corpus," *Journal of Peace Education* 11, no. 2 (2014): 181–207. This research was made possible thanks to a generous research grant of the US Institute for Peace.

31 Hillel Cohen, *Good Arabs: The Israeli Security Agencies and the Israeli Arabs, 1948–1967* (Berkeley: University of California Press, 2010); Elia Zureik, David Lyon, and Yasmeen Abu-Laban, *Surveillance and Control in Israel/Palestine: Population, Territory, and Power* (London: Routledge, 2011); Ahmad H. Sa'adi, "Afterword: Reflections on Representation, History and Moral Accountability," in: *Nakba: Palestine, 1948, and the Claims of Memory*, ed. Ahmad H. Sa'di and Lila Abu-Lughod (New York: Columbia University Press, 2007), 285–314; Internet source; I. Makkawi, "Role Conflict and the Dilemma of Palestinian Teachers in Israel," *Comparative Education* 39, no. 1 (2002): 39–52; I. Abu-Saad, "Palestinian Education in Israel: The Legacy of the Military Government," *Holy Land Studies* 5, no. 1 (2006): 21–56.

32 Yehouda Shenhav, "The Sociologists and the Occupation," *Israeli Sociology* 9, no. 2 (2008): 263–70. [Hebrew]

6 This Is Not "Co-Hummus"

1 Effi Ziv, "Insidious Trauma," *Mafteach* 5 (2002): 44–55. [Hebrew]

2 R. Halabi and N. Sonnenschein, "The Jewish-Palestinian Encounter in a Time of Crisis," *Journal of Social Issues* 6, no. 2 (2004): 373–87.

3 Nadim Rouhana and H. C. Kelman, "Promoting Joint Thinking in International Conflicts: An Israeli-Palestinian Continuing Workshop," *Journal of Social Issues* 50, no. 1 (1994): 157–78; N. Schimmel, "Towards a Sustainable and Holistic Model of Peace Education: A Critique of Conventional Modes of Peace Education through Dialogue in Israel," *Journal of Peace Education* 6, no. 1 (2009): 51–68.

4   Y. Maoz, "Peace Building in Violent Conflict: Israeli-Palestinian Post-Oslo People-to-People Activities," *International Journal of Politics, Culture and Society* 17, no. 3 (2004): 563–74.

5   M. Abu-Nimer, "Education for Coexistence and Arab-Jewish Encounters in Israel: Potential and Challenges," *Journal of Social Issues* 60, no. 2 (2004): 405–22.

6   Daphna Golan-Agnon, *Next Year in Jerusalem: Everyday Life in a Divided Land* (New York: New Press, 2005).

7   Albert Memmi, *The Colonizer and the Colonized* (Boston: Beacon Press, 1965).

8   Dafna Hirsch, "Hummus Is Best When It Is Fresh and Made by Arabs": The Gourmetization of Hummus in Israel and the Return of the Repressed Arab," *American Ethnologist* 38, no. 4 (2011): 617–30. https://doi.org/10.1111/j.1548-1425.2011.01326.x.

INDEX

electric & ordinary

ask Shul/Rafi for toothbrush, toothpaste, dental floss, WE newspaper,
2 book next to my bed